ignite

Ron Moore
Ps 18.28

ignite

Ron Moore

WinePress Publishing (PO Box 428, Enumclaw, WA 98022) functions only as book publisher. As such, the ultimate design, content, editorial accuracy, and views expressed or implied in this work are those of the author.

The author has made every effort to trace the ownership of all poems and quotes. In the event of a question arising from the use of a poem or quote, we regret any error made and will be pleased to make the necessary correction in future editions of this book.

Unless otherwise noted, all Scriptures are taken from the *Holy Bible, New International Version®, NIV®*. Copyright © 1973, 1978, 1984 by Biblica, Inc.™ Used by permission of Zondervan. All rights reserved worldwide. WWW.ZONDERVAN.COM

Scripture quotations marked NLT are taken from the *Holy Bible, New Living Translation*, copyright © 1996. Used by permission of Tyndale House Publishers, Inc., Wheaton, Illinois 60189. All rights reserved.

ISBN 13: 978-1-60615-002-3
ISBN 10: 1-60615-002-2
Library of Congress Catalog Card Number: 2009920565

Contents

Chapter 1

What an entrance he made! . . . He came into the darkness of my heart and turned on the light. He built a fire in the cold hearth and banished the chill. . . . I have never regretted opening the door to Christ and I never will.

—Robert Boyd Munger
My Heart—Christ's Home

There's a fire on the third floor! Where are the kids?"

Up until that point of the evening, my wife, Lori, and I were enjoying a relaxing dinner and conversation with a missionary couple. A week of exciting and exhausting ministry—a team from our church had traveled to the southeast coast of Spain to lead a conference—was winding down. Then Lara, a missionary attending the conference, burst through the doors and announced the fire.

We scattered from the table. Lori dashed one way and I raced the other, searching for our four children. When I couldn't find them inside the hotel, I headed outside to the pool area. On my way I saw billowing black smoke and orange flames shooting out of a third-story window. An explosion sent a ball of fire rolling out of the window and up into the sky. Hotel guests "oohed" and "aahed" as they herded their families away from the building.

Thankfully, within a few minutes, we found our children. We gathered by the Mediterranean Sea with the other people attending the conference. Behind us the waves crashed onto the rocky beach; in front of us the fire continued to burn. The hotel did not have a sprinkler system and the little resort city did not have a fire truck. We wondered how long the fire would burn seemingly out of control. Finally, a fire truck arrived from a neighboring city and the blaze was extinguished in short order.

Now, here's the amazing thing. The fire had burned for over an hour, but it never spread! The fire was contained in one small room where paper and cleaning supplies were stored. In many hotels that fire would have moved quickly throughout the building, causing major damage. But in this Spanish hotel constructed of tile and stucco, the fire was contained to that one small storage area.

SPREADING THE FIRE

Years ago Robert Boyd Munger wrote a great little book titled *My Heart—Christ's Home*. In this booklet, which has impacted the lives of hundreds of thousands of believers, Munger challenged his readers to imagine Jesus coming into the home of our heart. Munger recounted the night he invited Christ into his heart:

> What an entrance he made! It was not a spectacular, emotional thing, but very real, occurring at the very center of my soul. He came into the darkness of my heart and turned on the light. He built a fire in

2

the cold hearth and banished the chill. He started music where there had been stillness and harmony where there had been discord. He filled the emptiness with his own living fellowship. I have never regretted opening the door to Christ and I never will.[1]

In his story Munger and Jesus took a tour of his heart, Christ's new home. Jesus instructed the new believer to keep the "study of the mind" packed "full with the Word of God." Jesus was offered a standing invitation to the dining room, where appetites and desires were kept. Munger used the living room to explain the need for fellowship with Christ. The workroom was the place where Christ used our gifts and abilities for eternal purposes. Jesus was not to be left out of the recreational room, where hobbies and leisure occupied spare time. Munger didn't banish Jesus from the bedroom, the place of sexual purity. And, of course, the closets, where hidden sins were kept, needed to be cleaned out. Munger ended his challenging words with the owner signing over the deed.

> Running as fast as I could to the strong-box, I took out the deed to the house describing its assets and liabilities, its condition, location, and situation. Then rushing back to him, I eagerly signed it over giving title to him alone for time and eternity. "Here it is, all that I am and have forever. Now you run the house. . . ."[2]

Munger's booklet is a challenging reminder of the profound power of following God with our whole heart. Certainly, this is (or should be) the deepest desire of every believer. We want nothing more than for God to take charge of our lives. We want him to control every room. We know that surrendering our heart to Christ will be the only thing that brings a deep personal sense of meaning and the only way we can truly honor God. John Piper says it well: "God is most glorified in us when we are most satisfied in him."[3]

Back to that Hotel Fire

It has been my privilege in twenty years of ministry to partner with some very committed believers. They understand that Christ is to rule over every area of their heart. But even when we give the "title to him alone for time and eternity," even when the fire is burning in our hearts, life still comes at us fast. I believe far too many believers live with a warm fire burning in the hearth of the heart, keeping the "chill" away but not allowing that fire to spread into the inevitable challenges and struggles that barge into their lives. Like the hotel in Spain, the fire that should consume is contained.

Too often we are like the Israelites, who experienced the power of God but seldom moved the power of God into their experience. They walked through the sea on dry ground and watched God destroy the pursuing Egyptians but days later couldn't trust God for food and water. We trust God for eternal salvation but can't trust him to meet us in the broken areas of our lives. We forget that wherever we are, whatever we are going through, God is already there.

God Meets Us Where We Are

God meets us right where we are. When the heavy fog of loneliness settles over our soul, he is there. He meets us in the midst of our failure, when pain and confusion have saturated every part of our lives. When our days are filled with unfulfilled dreams, unrequited prayers, unanswered questions, unsatisfied longings, unknown futures, and unmet expectations, there he stands. God embraces us in our disappointments and emptiness. God speaks to us when we are reeling from bad decisions that lead us to dire places. When we are broken he comes, not only to bandage the wounds, but to set our attentive hearts on fire. He is not content for us to limp; he wants us to leap! Our queries don't scare God away. He comes to turn our unanswered questions into unexplainable confidence. God meets us to ignite us! He connects with us in the events of our lives to ignite a burning passion to follow hard after him.

HEART FOR GOD—FEET OF CLAY

We need a guide for our journey together. We need someone who has met with God in real-life experience. I don't know about you, but I am wearied by those people who only share their success stories. I want to learn from a person who followed hard after God but also stumbled along the way. I can think of no better mentor in this process than David, the Old Testament king of Israel.

God called King David "a man after my own heart." I think you would agree that's a pretty high mark in the class of spiritual development. From the time he was a boy David walked with God. David experienced the eternal God working in and through his everyday life. He boldly took on larger-than-life foes "in the name of the Lord God Almighty." When others shrank back in fear, he stepped forward in confidence. Because the Lord was his "Shepherd" he had everything he wanted. Even when he walked through the valley of the shadow of death he felt God with him. David's ignited heart consumed his life experience.

David's heart beat with God's, but his feet were made of clay. David knew what it felt like to walk alone. He fell into sexual sin and lived through the painful consequences.

David experienced times when his heart was filled with questions and didn't hesitate to express them:

Be merciful to me, LORD, for I am faint; O LORD heal me, for my bones are in agony. My soul is in anguish. How long, O LORD, how long?
—Psalm 6:2–3

Why, O LORD, do you stand far off? Why do you hide yourself in times of trouble?
—Psalm 10:1

How long, O LORD? Will you forget me forever? How long will you hide your face from me? How long must I wrestle with my thoughts and every day have sorrow in my heart? How long will my enemy triumph over me?
—Psalm 13:1–2

My God, my God, why have you forsaken me? Why are you so far from saving me, so far from the words of my groaning?
—Psalm 22:1

At one point, the fatigue, after years of running from Saul, led David to join forces with Israel's sworn enemy. Bad decision! Once David and his men returned from battle to find their homes had been destroyed and their wives and children taken captive. "David and his men wept aloud until they had no strength to weep" (1 Sam. 30:4). Then David's men blamed him and planned to stone him.

And God answered every one of David's prayers. Sometimes the answer was "Yes," sometimes "Wait," and sometimes "No!"

David's heart for God and feet of clay make him a great guide for our journey. We will discover how David's heart burned for God and was not contained. The fire spread to ignite his loneliness, brokenness, disappointment, and emptiness. I believe we will find that David's story is our story. We will learn that spiritual growth seldom takes place in times of quiet reflection. Instead God most often ignites our hearts in the everyday experiences of life.

Father, we commit our journey to you. Our hearts are hardened unless you soften them. We are blinded unless you cause us to see. Open our ears so that we can hear your voice. Do your work, we pray.
In Christ's name.
Amen.

Chapter 2

Igniting a Heart in the Sheep Pens

> *The work of formation is to be found in the midst of all life and should never be sequestered to the cloister.*
> —Richard Foster

laise Pascal, the famous seventeenth-century French scientist, is often noted as one of the six greatest thinkers of all time. But Pascal was more than a man with a great mind; he was a man with a heart that beat in rhythm with God. One night Pascal had an overwhelming encounter with the living God. He recorded the experience on a piece of paper, folded it, and kept it in his pocket close to his heart. Those present at his death found the worn, creased paper with these words:

> From about half-past ten at night to about half-after midnight—fire! O God of Abraham, God of Isaac, God of Jacob—not the god of the philosophers and the wise. The God of Jesus Christ who can be known only in the ways of the Gospel. Security—feeling—peace—joy—tears of joy. Amen.[1]

No one knows exactly what happened to Pascal that night, but whatever it was, his heart was penetrated with "fire." God ignited his heart with security and peace. The "fire" penetrated his spiritual numbness and "feeling" returned—to the point that Pascal could not hold back the tears of joy. No wonder he recorded the experience and kept it close to his heart! When God ignites our hearts, it's something we never want to forget. Shouldn't every believer desire such a journey with God? Where does such a journey begin? Let's look at the Old Testament book of 1 Samuel for the answer.

THE PEOPLE WANTED A REALLY COOL KING

The people of Israel were tired of having an old prophet riding on a donkey as their leader. Influenced by other nations, they wanted a king who wore royal robes and rode in chariots flanked by soldiers. So . . . God gave them the king they desired and deserved. His name was Saul. The people chose him because of his impressive appearance. Saul stood a head taller than all the rest (1 Sam. 10:23). But unfortunately, Saul had a heart problem. His public life was characterized by imprudence, jealousy, impatience, and an inability to admit and deal with failure. Eventually, God rejected Saul and sent the prophet Samuel to find his replacement.

Samuel's assignment took him off the beaten path to a little town called Bethlehem. This was the first, but not the last, time that this little village would play a significant role in God's plan. God directed Samuel to a man named Jesse and told the prophet, "I have chosen one of his sons to be king" (1 Sam. 16:1). Saul was the people's choice, but God hand-picked his successor.

After bypassing Jesse's first seven sons, Samuel asked if he had any other sons. "'There is still the youngest,' Jesse answered, 'but he is tending the sheep'" (1 Sam. 16:11).

Admittedly, the scouting report for number eight was weak. The last of Jesse's sons was young and unproven. His leadership experience was limited to leading a flock of sheep from one grazing area to another. That's why Jesse didn't even call him in from the field when Samuel wanted to meet with his sons. But after Samuel finally saw him, God told Samuel, "Rise and anoint him; he is the one" (1 Sam. 16:12).

God cuts through the externals; the young shepherd was a man after God's own heart. He loved the things God loved. He hated the things God hated. He shared the burdens of God's heart. How does that happen? How did God ignite this young man's heart?

THE KING FROM THE SHEEP PENS

Psalm 78 gives a poetic history of Israel, beginning with Jacob and running all the way through Saul's reign. Then the psalmist introduces the new king. It's not quite the fanfare you might expect for royalty, so get ready to be unimpressed:

> He chose David his servant and took him from the
> sheep pens; from tending the sheep he brought him
> to be the shepherd of his people Jacob, of Israel
> his inheritance. And David shepherded them with
> integrity of heart; with skillful hands he led them.
> —Psalm 78:70–72

The serene image of David sitting on a beautiful hillside, a gentle breeze blowing through his hair on a sunshiny day as he played his harp and sang the Twenty-Third Psalm takes a beating when we learn that God found David in the "sheep

11

pens." Shepherding was hard, odorous, dirty work. Shepherds rose early to lead the sheep through mountain passes to grazing pastures. They stayed up late to protect the sheep from wild animals. Shepherds went after the strays that wandered away. They freed the lamb that was caught in a thicket. They put salve on the sheep's noses to keep the flies away. They tended wounds. Then they brought the sheep back into the pens for winter. It was lonely, dangerous, and difficult work. But God used that experience to ignite David's heart and prepare him for his life's work.

God does the same for us. Some events in our lives will be as joyful and satisfying as writing the Twenty-Third Psalm was for David. There will be times of spiritual elation. Spiritual blessings will result in mountaintop experiences. But don't get used to the altitude. We will, at some point or another, return to the lowlands.

Some assignments will be very difficult. Some events will stretch us. Some days will be painful. Brokenness will not be a stranger. Loneliness will be a brief visitor for some and a long-term houseguest for others. Disappointment will show up without an invitation. And we will spend more time than we desire waiting . . . and waiting . . . and waiting. All of us will have our sheep pens, but don't forget that when you are lonely, you are never alone; when you are broken, you have not been cast off; when you are disappointed, you have not been forgotten; and when you are waiting, there is One who waits patiently with you. He ignites our hearts when we let him work in the sheep pens of our lives.

God Does His Best Work in Our "Sheep Pens"

Surely, God sets his people's hearts on fire as they meet with him in extended times of solitude. He ignites us in times of prayer and fasting. And don't cancel your spiritual retreats.

Times of solitude, fasting, and retreats are needed and should be scheduled by all believers. But I believe that a burning passion is lit and kindled in the midst of everyday life. I believe God does his work during 4:00 A.M. feedings, potty training, sprints to the bus stop, and carpooling kids to practice. I believe God is striking the spiritual match when we are stretching budgets to make ends meet, writing checks for another car repair, and contemplating career changes. I believe God does some of his best work when we are maneuvering through economic turmoil, dealing with the disappointment of missed opportunities, cultivating relationships, struggling with disconnection in marriage, and working through a conflict with a friend. I don't know about you, but my life is not one long worship service singing all the songs I love. I spend most of my time in the hard, dirty, difficult challenges of life. Life is not one long devotional time.

Never "Sequestered to the Cloister"

Richard Foster is one of the most well known writers in the area of spiritual disciplines. His book *Celebration of Discipline* introduced many evangelical Christians to the disciplines of fasting, solitude, simplicity, and silence. In a recent interview Foster was asked how all these disciplines worked when he was in the midst of the busyness of raising a family. Foster's response is quite instructive:

> The work of formation is to be found in the midst of all life and should never be sequestered to the cloister. The two major places where spiritual formation should work, and where the disciplines are vital elements, are the home—children, family—and work. Those are the two places where most of our lives are spent.

I often counsel mothers, for example, who have their little ones they are nursing that they shouldn't try to do retreats. When they are nursing their children, that's the time of prayer. What better metaphor for the transference of the life of God to us than a mother with a baby? Or when you're playing with your kids—that's the laughter of God. You discover God *in* that and not outside of it.[2]

In the midst of David's lonely, thankless, hard work, God ignited the future leader's heart. David learned how to shepherd sheep and then took the transferable principles to people. He developed a heart of integrity when there was no one around to impress. That same heart of integrity led a nation to greatness. The skills of nurturing, protecting, and caring for sheep became the skills David used as king. God called David from the pens to the palace.

Are you letting God into your sheep pens? Are you inviting him to meet you in your job loss, economic anxiety, break-up, and illness? Yeah, I know sometimes they stink! I know that it's not where you want to be or thought you would be. You may feel alone and abandoned. You may be discouraged. You may feel like you have been placed on hold. But you have to know this: God is not wasting your time. Don't waste his. Let him prepare you for your future. God does his best heart work in the hard work of "sheep pens."

SHEEP PENS AND FOCUS

My most dangerous times are unfocused times. Pursuits, activities, and responsibilities—all good in and of themselves—pull me in many different directions. More often than I'd like to admit it, these unfocused times result in priority flip-flop. C. H. Spurgeon said it this way: "Divided aims tend to distraction, weakness, and disappointment." I have experienced that to be true.

The sheep pens of David's life led him to focus on "one thing":

> One thing I ask of the LORD, this is what I seek: that I may dwell in the house of the LORD all the days of my life, to gaze upon the beauty of the LORD and to seek him in his temple.
>
> —Psalm 27:4

This singular endeavor was David's deep desire and his active quest. The sheep pens developed a desire for a heart ignited with a burning passion to follow hard after God all the days of his life. David was not content to simply read about God or think about God or talk about God. He wanted to live life with God. He wanted to actively seek the Lord. He desired to live in God's presence. David was determined to experience God's beauty and majesty.

An ignited heart is not "sequestered to a cloister." The fire burns in the normal activities of life. It is a focused fire, with penetrating heat that burns with a passionate desire to follow God in the twists and turns, up the mountains and down the valleys of this journey we call life. And whether we are running at full speed or standing still to catch our breath, whether we are carefully positioning our feet for the climb or maneuvering the steep descent, we have this "one thing"—prayer. O God, let the fire burn.

DAVID'S FIRST ASSIGNMENT

God often prescribes an interesting training regimen. David had passed the test in the sheep pens. Now, a new educational program began in the palace. Saul had been imprudent; God's assignment for David was purposed to produce godly wisdom. Saul was filled with envy; God was looking for David to show contentment in a difficult circumstance. Saul had made rash decisions; God was watching to see if David was ready to depend on him. A few days away at a spiritual retreat would have been easier. But God wanted to see David's heart in action.

I WANT TO SEE YOUR HEART

Several years ago, a person sent me an e-mail about a man named John Blanchard who found a book in a library that intrigued him. Actually, he was more impressed with the notes that were penciled into the margins of the book. The soft handwriting and thoughtful words reflected an insightful mind and a tender heart. Turning to the front of the book, he discovered that a Miss Hollis Maynell had donated it to the library.

That knowledge propelled a quest. With dogged determination he acquired her address. He wrote a letter of introduction and invited her to correspond. The next day he was shipped overseas for service in World War II. The two corresponded for the next year and felt a romance beginning. Blanchard requested a photograph, but she refused. If he really cared, she reasoned, it wouldn't matter what she looked like. When the day finally came for him to return from Europe, they scheduled a meeting for 7:00 P.M. at Grand Central Station.

"How will I find you?" he asked.

"You'll recognize me by the red rose I'll be wearing on my lapel."

At 7:00 P.M. sharp, John Blanchard stood in the crowded station, looking for a girl whose heart he loved, but whose face he'd never seen. Blanchard tells what happened:

> A young woman was coming toward me, her figure long and slim. Her blonde hair lay back in curls

from her delicate ears; her eyes were blue as flowers. Her lips and chin had a gentle firmness, and in her pale green suit she was like springtime come alive. I started toward her, entirely forgetting to notice that she was not wearing a rose. As I moved, a small, provocative smile curved her lips. "Going my way, sailor?" she asked. Almost uncontrollably I made one step closer to her . . . and then I saw Hollis Maynell. She was standing almost directly behind the girl. A woman well past forty with graying hair tucked under a worn hat. She was more than plump, her thick-ankled feet thrust into low-heeled shoes.

The girl in the green suit was walking quickly away. I felt as though I were split in two. So keen was my desire to follow her, and yet so deep was my longing for the woman whose spirit had truly companioned me and upheld my own. And there she stood. Her pale, plump face was gentle and sensible; her gray eyes had a warm and kindly twinkle. I did not hesitate. My fingers gripped the small worn leather copy of the book that was to identify me to her. This would not be love, but it would be something precious, something perhaps even better than love; a friendship for which I had been and must ever be grateful.

I squared my shoulders and saluted. I held out the book to the woman, even though while I spoke I felt choked by the bitterness of my disappointment. "I'm Lieutenant John Blanchard, and you must be Miss Maynell. I am so glad you could meet me. May I take you to dinner?" The woman's face broadened into a tolerant smile. "I don't know what this is about, son," she answered, "but the young lady in the green suit who just went by, she begged me to wear this rose on my coat. She said if you ask me out to dinner, I should tell you that she is waiting for you in the big restaurant across the street. She said it was some kind of a test."[3]

Hollis was wise beyond her years. She wanted to see John Blanchard's heart in action. That's what God is looking for—a heart that acts in line with his. And he isn't opposed to putting us to the test to find out.

God chose David from the sheep pens, anointed him king, and gave him his first royal assignment: serve the king by playing your harp to soothe his nerves. But quite honestly, a few tunes on the harp would not be the new king's toughest assignment. Not long after holding the harp, David held the head of the giant Goliath (1 Sam. 17). That conquest launched him to rock star status overnight. He was on the cover of Israel's "50 Most Beautiful People." He became the country's most eligible bachelor. Ballads were written of David's feats and sung by the young maidens.

David said, "This is great!" God said, "David, things are moving a little too fast. Let's slow down. You have a lot to learn before you wear the crown."

For the next ten years, God put David on the run. A jealous Saul, who still thought he was king, chased David up the mountains and through the valleys. During that decade, God took David through the fire so the flames would engulf his whole heart.

Spiritual exercises and inspiring sermons provide great sparks, but they can never set our whole heart ablaze. Ignited hearts are a result of on-the-job training. The assignments will be hard. The classes will last longer than we would like. The tuition is not cheap. But the degree is priceless! When your whole heart is ignited by God, there is nothing else in life that even comes close to that experience.

Invite God into your sheep pens. He will meet you there and ignite your heart with a burning passion to follow hard after him.

> *Father, I want it now; teach me to wait. I want it on my terms; prepare me for yours. I want the growth without the "sheep pens." Help me understand that the growth I really want only takes place in difficult places. Give me a heart committed to on-the-job training. Give me the courage of commitment. Ignite my heart with a burning passion to follow hard after you.*
> *In Jesus' name.*
> *Amen.*

Chapter 3

Igniting a Lonely Heart

> *Two are better than one, because they have a good*
> *return for their work: If one falls down, his friend can*
> *help him up. But pity the man who falls and has no*
> *one to help him up!*
>
> —Ecclesiastes 4:9

Remember the song that John Lennon and Paul McCartney wrote back in 1966 about a woman named Eleanor Rigby? You probably know the tune. It paints a sad picture of a woman who lived and died alone. She hid her loneliness well by keeping a mask in a jar by the door. In private she lived alone in her loneliness. But when she walked out the door she put on the pretense of self-sufficiency and independence.

Meanwhile, a priest named Father Mackenzie stood in the pulpit of Eleanor's church and preached to people who were simply present to fulfill their religious duty. They didn't care about what he had to say. So Father Mackenzie lived a meaningless life of preparing sermons that no one listened to. Eleanor experienced loneliness in the confines of her home.

Mackenzie experienced his loneliness on the stage in front of his parishioners.

Can you relate to Eleanor Rigby or Father Mackenzie? Is your heart lonely? Maybe you hide it well. Like Eleanor, you wear a mask, or like Mackenzie, you just keep on with your life's work although the futility continues to highlight the hole in your heart. You don't feel like you can let others know you are actually hurting or you don't have it all together. So when you venture out you put on that mask you keep in a jar by the door, or go on pretending from the "pulpit" that your life carries meaning. All this takes a lot of work, doesn't it?

I was recently interviewed on a television show. Before the interview, the producer told me what time I needed to be in the makeup room. I have a friend who does sports broadcasting, and he refuses to do the makeup thing. So I told my daughter about the gig and the makeup appointment. I told her that, like my broadcasting friend, I was going to refuse the makeup. After I had finished explaining my plan she looked at me and said without hesitation, "Dad, you need the makeup. Do the makeup!" So after an uncomfortable time in the makeup room, I went on the set feeling a bit like Eleanor. I'm sure I looked better on the outside . . . but that makeup didn't do a thing for my heart.

LONELINESS COMES IN
DIFFERENT SHAPES AND SIZES

It is easy to understand the loneliness that we can experience when we are isolated from others. But we can also experience loneliness even when we are surrounded by other people.

Physical Loneliness

Some people live their lives alone. Mother Teresa said, "The most terrible poverty is loneliness and the feeling of being unloved." Some people never find the right mate. Others go solo due to the pain of a past experience. Who wants to hurt like that again? Sometimes death takes those we love. Sometimes divorce leaves us alone and serves as a constant reminder of what we once had and wanted.

A few years ago a group from our church went to a nursing home to sing some Christmas hymns with the residents. After the singing was over, I spoke with several of the people. I will never forget one woman's story. She was engaged to be married and had taken a business trip to another state. When she returned her fiancé was scheduled to pick her up at the airport. But he never made it. He was killed in a car accident on the way to get her. She never married, and now she sat alone in a nursing home with the few memories of a short relationship and the imagined memories of a life that might have been.

Emotional Loneliness

Some people are never physically alone. They surround themselves with people, but behind the beer and pretzels, below the surface talk and surface relationships, beyond the group Bible studies, there is a deep emotional loneliness. This is not about being an introvert or extrovert. This type of loneliness exists in people who have a deep emotional need that can't quite be filled.

In a 2007 study, George Barna found that adults, especially those under thirty years old, strive to develop relationships with a large number of people, and yet the study found that even so, they continue to live with a sense of loneliness and isolation. Barna reports,

The constant involvement with social networking via the Internet, text messaging and phone calls via mobile devices, and frequent appearances at common hangouts (think Starbucks®, movie theaters, and favorite restaurants) are manifestations of the investment in relationships that are important but somehow not as fulfilling as desired.[1]

"We're born alone, we live alone, we die alone," noted Orson Welles. Then he added, "Only through our love and friendship can we create the illusion for the moment that we're not alone."

Positional Loneliness

Leadership can be a very lonely place. Sure, you work to build a team. You interact with others. You listen and assimilate information. But at the end of the day you have to make decisions—tough decisions that impact others. I will never forget sitting in the office of a top-level team member discussing a difficult situation that was going to impact a lot of people. He gave me his counsel and input and then said, "At the end of the day, you are the only one who can make this decision." That was a lonely realization. Everyone who serves at the top of an organization knows it is a lonely place.

A few years ago, Fred Smith addressed this issue in the *Leadership Journal*. Smith said,

> Years ago, I spoke to a group of presidents in Columbus, Ohio, about loneliness in leadership. One participant, president of an architectural firm, came up afterward and said, "You've solved my problem." "What's your problem?" I asked. "My organization's always confused," he said, "and I didn't know why. It's because I don't like to be

lonely; I've got to talk about my ideas to the rest of the company. But they never know which ones will work, so everybody who likes my idea jumps to work on it. Those who don't, work against it. Employees are going backward and forward—when the idea may not even come about at all." Fearing loneliness, this president was not able to keep his ideas to himself until they were better formulated. A leader must be able to keep his or her own counsel until the proper time.[2]

King David understood and experienced physical, emotional, and positional loneliness. As a shepherd he experienced many days and nights by himself tending to the needs of sheep. For the first ten years of his kingship, David was on the run from Saul. Many times he ran alone. David's emotional aloneness is seen time and again as he poured out his heart to God. David pleaded with God,

> Turn to me and be gracious to me, for I am lonely and afflicted. The troubles of my heart have multiplied; free me from my anguish.
> —Psalm 25:16–17

Later we will consider a time when all of David's men turned against him and threatened to stone him. But God provided a remedy for David, and I believe he has a remedy for you. God desires to penetrate the walls of loneliness with true biblical community.

We Were Made to Live in Community

God said, "It is not good for the man to be alone" (Gen. 2:18). We were created for community. Solomon understood this well and explained why two are better than one.

> Two are better than one, because they have a good
> return for their work: If one falls down, his friend
> can help him up. But pity the man who falls and
> has no one to help him up! Also, if two lie down to-
> gether, they will keep warm. But how can one keep
> warm alone? Though one may be overpowered, two
> can defend themselves. A cord of three strands is
> not quickly broken.
>
> —Ecclesiastes 4:9–12

We were made to be in communion with others. The return on our effort is better. There is someone to help us to
our feet when we take one of life's inevitable falls. There is
warmth and comfort in godly friendships. There is protection.
When lives are wrapped together, our weaknesses are covered
by each other's strengths. We are made to employ our abilities,
resources, and time to make a spiritual impact on those around
us. Interacting with one another in biblical community is a
major theme of Scripture.

- Be devoted to one another in brotherly love (Rom. 12:10a).
- Honor one another above yourselves (Rom. 12:10b).
- Live in harmony with one another (Rom. 12:16).
- Love one another (Rom. 13:8).
- Don't pass judgment on one another (Rom. 14:13).
- Accept one another (Rom. 15:7).
- Greet one another with a holy kiss (Rom. 16:16)—Careful!
- Serve one another in love (Gal. 5:13).
- Be patient and bear with one another in love (Eph. 4:2).
- Be kind and compassionate to one another (Eph. 4:32a).

- Forgive each other just as in Christ God forgave you (Eph. 4:32b).
- Submit to one another out of reverence for Christ (Eph. 5:21).
- Teach and admonish one another (Col. 3:16).
- Encourage one another and build each other up (1 Thess. 5:11).
- Spur one another on toward love and good deeds (Heb. 10:24).
- Offer hospitality to one another without grumbling (1 Peter 4:9).

This is not an exhaustive list but I think you get the idea. "One-anothering" is hard to do when we aren't involved with other people. We need others in our life who are going in the same direction, at the same time, for the same reason. David experienced this kind of rich community with a friend named Jonathan.

FINDING THE SAME HEARTBEAT

God called David from the sheep pens and anointed him king of Israel. Overnight David began enjoying rock star status. He killed Goliath and led the nation in victorious battles. Songs were written about him. He married Saul's daughter, Michal. Not bad for a young man yet to see his twentieth birthday. But in the midst of the sunshine, there were a few sprinkles of rain. David's father-in-law, the former king who thought that he was the present king, kept a jealous eye on David. Kings are not fond of rivals and Saul wasted no time to act. Saul told his son Jonathan and all his attendants to kill David. But instead of killing David, Jonathan warned him of Saul's intentions and then devised a plan to protect him.

"I will go out and stand with my father in the field where you are. I'll speak to him about you and will tell you what I find out." Jonathan spoke well of David to Saul his father and said to him, "Let not the king do wrong to his servant David; he has not wronged you, and what he has done has benefited you greatly. He took his life in his hands when he killed the Philistine. The LORD won a great victory for all Israel, and you saw it and were glad. Why then would you do wrong to an innocent man like David by killing him for no reason?" Saul listened to Jonathan and took this oath: "As surely as the LORD lives, David will not be put to death."

—1 Samuel 19:3–6

David was excited to hear the good news and returned to serve Saul, but the king still had some issues. One night as David was playing the harp to soothe Saul, he looked up to see Saul's arm cocked and a spear coming toward his head. David ducked just in time. With the spear still vibrating in the wall, he headed for the hills.

Through a series of events, Jonathan helped David escape death. But I always wondered, "Why?" Jonathan was next in line for the crown. Why would Jonathan befriend the man who would keep him from sitting on the king's throne? To answer that question, let's go back to 1 Samuel 18 and see how this friendship started.

Under Saul's leadership, Israel was completely dominated by the Philistines. In fact, to prevent the Israelites from making weapons of war, the Philistines would not even allow a blacksmith in Israelite territory. Discouragement and despair hung over the nation like an ominous storm cloud. Then it got worse. Israel woke up one day to find that the Philistines were bored with just oppressing them—they wanted to annihilate them.

At this point in the game, Saul was down to about six hundred men and some homemade weapons. Things were looking pretty bleak. So Jonathan took matters into his own hands. He told his armor-bearer:

> "Come, let's go over to the outpost of those uncircumcised fellows. Perhaps the LORD will act in our behalf. Nothing can hinder the LORD from saving, whether by many or by few."
> "Do all that you have in mind," his armor-bearer said. "Go ahead; I am with you heart and soul."
> —1 Samuel 14:6–7

Though he knew the Philistines were waiting at the top, Jonathan, convinced that the Lord was with him, climbed the cliff. In the space of half an acre, he and his armor-bearer, empowered by the Spirit of God, killed twenty Philistines. God caused the Philistines to panic, and the rest of Israel's army joined in to rout the enemy. The victory was led by Jonathan's trust and confidence in the God of heaven and earth.

Three chapters later, the Philistines regrouped behind their leader—a ten-foot giant named Goliath. He challenged any Israelite man to a one-on-one battle, winner take all. For forty days Goliath taunted, teased, and ridiculed the Israelite army. Each day they trembled and retreated. And Jonathan was among the tremblers and retreaters. His once confident heart was filled with fear. Jonathan had been so confident in God's strength that he scaled a cliff and killed twenty skilled warriors. Now he ran, like the rest, from one Philistine. Think of the turmoil that must have been going on in Jonathan's heart—faith battling fear, confidence wrestling cowardice, the desire to stand strong melting into the reality of retreat.

On day number forty-one, Goliath came forward again. Certain this day would be like the previous ones, he confidently spewed his mocking defiance. But this day was different. God presented an unlikely opponent, a young man from the sheep pens. Jonathan stood nearby when Saul tried to stop David from fighting Goliath—telling him that he was too young and inexperienced. Jonathan's heart must have leaped when he heard David tell Saul:

> Your servant has been keeping his father's sheep. When a lion or a bear came and carried off a sheep from the flock, I went after it, struck it and rescued the sheep from its mouth. When it turned on me, I seized it by its hair, struck it and killed it. Your servant has killed both the lion and the bear; this uncircumcised Philistine will be like one of them, because he has defied the armies of the living God. The LORD who delivered me from the paw of the lion and the paw of the bear will deliver me from the hand of this Philistine.
>
> —1 Samuel 17:34–37

Just as Jonathan scaled that cliff in complete trust, so David went against Goliath and returned victorious. After that amazing encounter David stood before Saul again, this time holding Goliath's bloody head, and Jonathan saw a person whose heart beat with his. "Jonathan became one in spirit with David, and he loved him as himself" (1 Sam. 18:1). They shared the same purpose for life and the same passion for God. They were headed in the same direction with the same priorities. They longed for the same things. They dreamed the same dreams. They knew that taking on a task without God was foolish. So God penetrated their hearts to burn with true friendship.

Until this point David lived life alone. The youngest of the family, he was out tending the sheep when God sent Samuel to change the course of his life. He went to the battlefield alone. After Goliath, David did not return to his family. He rose quickly in popularity and position. Success can be one of the loneliest places on earth. So God ignited David's heart with a true friend.

The friendship between David and Jonathan was one of kindred spirit. The bond they shared was a healthy, deep, and binding love based on passion for God and his will for their lives. It was a love stronger than blood, deeper than royal privilege, and threaded with a true sense of mutual care. They had each other's backs.

Jonathan's heart for David was amazing. A live David meant Jonathan would never sit on the throne. His love for David was sacrificial. He was willing to step aside so David could step to the front. Jonathan knew that neither tradition nor lineage could stand in God's way. He was determined to obey God rather than men.

EVERYBODY NEEDS A FRIEND

Recently I met with a group of singles in our church. Some had never been married. Others were divorced. Some had experienced the death of a spouse. My desire was to better understand the issues going on in their lives so that we could provide more effective ministry for them. I was pleased when an overflow crowd gathered in our café. We ordered mochas and lattes and began a lively discussion. I framed our time with five questions:

- As a single what does a fulfilled life in Christ look like?
- As you live in this present culture what are your greatest concerns?
- As you live in this present culture what are your greatest challenges?

- What has the church done/or is the church doing to help you live a fulfilled life in Christ in this culture?
- Where are we failing in ministering to the concerns and challenges of living as a single in our culture?

Woven in and through all the responses was the issue of loneliness. One man who was present and vocal was a friend of mine named Jim.

Jim is one of the most gregarious people you will ever meet. He always has a story. When I see Jim talking to a group of people in our church lobby, I tell them, "When you get tired of listening, just walk away. About ten minutes later he'll stop talking." We have that kind of relationship. I won't tell you what he says about me.

Jim's first wife left the family when his two children were young. He raised them as a single parent and then remarried about twelve years later. Jim's second wife died of a brain tumor. So Jim has known the pain of divorce and the grief of losing a spouse. He also understands the challenges of being a single parent.

Jim attended the singles meeting and I was struck by his openness. He spoke of his desire for Christian friendship and companionship. He told the story of flying a fighter jet through the Grand Canyon and the awesomeness of the experience. "Do you know what I wanted to do?" Jim asked the group. "I wanted to land the plane, get my friends, and take them up with me. It was an awesome experience, but I needed someone to share it with." Jim teaches at a college in our area and noted that he could retire. Then he added, "But why would I want to do that? I enjoy interacting with the students." In another vulnerable moment, Jim told the group about his love for the outdoors and for cycling the beautiful trails of western Pennsylvania. "I have 12,000 miles on my bike," Jim said, "but I have parked it. I have vowed never to ride again—alone."

Jim's candidness about his loneliness struck a chord with the singles. They were nodding in agreement. Others shared how they struggled and dealt with the issue. Loneliness was a common challenge for the group I met with that night.

Whether your loneliness is physical, emotional, or stems from your position, God ignites the lonely heart with true friendship. It may be one person or two or even three. But God desires to bring people into your life who share the same purpose and passion for God. Acquaintances are a dime a dozen. Many people consider themselves companions. True friendship, however, is deep, meaningful, and satisfying. How does a person find such a friend?

DEVELOPING BIBLICAL FRIENDSHIP

Developing real friendships does not happen overnight. Friendships take time, patience, and sacrifice. Here are some things to keep in mind as you work to develop biblical friendship.

Find Others Committed to Christ

Deep, biblical friendship starts with people who are committed to Christ. The instruction of Scripture is clear: "Do not be yoked together with unbelievers. For what do righteousness and wickedness have in common? Or what fellowship can light have with darkness?" (2 Cor. 6:14). A person who is walking in the darkness cannot direct you to passages in the Bible during trying circumstances; he cannot join you in prayer; and he cannot help you follow hard after Jesus. Proverbs 27:17 says, "As iron sharpens iron, so one man sharpens another." An unbeliever cannot sharpen you spiritually. I am not saying to forsake all non-Christian acquaintances. Keep building relationships with unbelievers so you can tell them about Jesus.

But for spiritual encouragement and accountability, your arms must be locked with those heading in the same spiritual direction and on the same spiritual page.

Men with Men and Women with Women

It seems too basic, but then again . . . . For those who are married, biblical friendship must be a man with a man and a woman with a woman. A deep friendship with a member of the opposite sex (other than a spouse) is inappropriate and foolish.

If you are married, don't let friendship outside your marriage infringe on the relationship between you and your spouse. Don't look to receive that deep level of emotional intimacy from anyone other than your mate. We will discuss friendship within marriage later in the chapter.

Don't Try to Force Friendship

Don't expect "soul bonding" overnight. You need to have some things in common. And true friendship takes time.

Pray for Opportunities

A friend of mine loves to do one-on-one discipleship. At a recent retreat he decided to sit by himself and pray that God would lead a person to him who needed a friend and desired to get engaged in Bible study. The first guy who visited him was interested but too busy. Then God arranged his appointment. An individual came and sat down who didn't know anyone at the retreat. They struck up a conversation that led to a relationship. They have been meeting regularly now for several months. It's amazing what God will do if we ask.

Place Yourself in Friendship Situations

You can't just pray for a friend and stay in your little cocoon. You need to find a community of believers and get involved. You are not going to find the friend you're looking for at the neighborhood bar or this month's coolest hangout. Biblical friendship is developed within biblical communities.

Take Off Your Mask

You have to find a place to be vulnerable and mask-less. The best place for this to happen is within the context of a small group. In time you will develop enough trust with others to reveal your heart to them. But remember, friendship is not about rubber stamp approval. A good friend is honest enough to point out flaws and blind spots even when it hurts. Proverbs 27:6 says, "Wounds from a friend can be trusted, but an enemy multiplies kisses."

Work at Being a Friend

One time, a person made a point to tell me how unfriendly our church was. Then I watched him one weekend as he stood alone by a wall with a scowl on his face. He might as well have been wearing a sign that said, "Stay Away!" It may be hard for you—as it was for him—to connect with people, but you need to at least appear as if you want to enter into conversation. Stretch yourself. You'll be glad you did.

A farmer was working by the side of a dirt road when a car slowed and came to a stop beside him. "We're moving to that town up ahead," the driver said and then asked, "Is it friendly?" Before answering the question, the wise farmer prodded for some background information. "Well . . ." he paused, taking off his hat and scratching his head, "tell me about the town you came from. How'd you get along there? Was it friendly?"

This time, the woman sitting on the passenger side, presumably the driver's wife, spoke up and gave the farmer an earful. "It was a terrible place to live," she said, closing her eyes and shaking her head. "The people were rude, critical, and narrow-minded. That's one of the reasons we left." "Hmm, I see, I see," said the farmer, nodding. "Well, I expect that you'll find the town up ahead to be just like the town you left."

In the words of the country song, "Wherever you go, there you are." You may find a great biblical community that understands the importance of building true biblical friendships. But if you are not willing to work at being friendly, you will continue in your loneliness. Work at being a friend by being friendly.

Be an Encourager

Mark Twain said, "I can live for two months on one compliment." The apostle Paul tells us to "encourage one another and build each other up" (1 Thess. 5:11). The writer of the book of Hebrews instructs us to "encourage one another daily" so that we will not become "hardened by sin's deceitfulness" (3:13). He emphasizes the importance of encouragement within biblical community when he writes, "Let us not give up meeting together, as some are in the habit of doing, but let us encourage one another—and all the more as you see the Day approaching" (10:25). If you encourage others, you'll find yourself surrounded by encouragers.

Practice Hospitality

Invite people into your home. Share a meal together. Enjoy an evening of fellowship. If you don't feel like you have the gift of hospitality, take someone out to eat. Or just buy him or her a cup of coffee or stop by a Sonic Drive-In® during Happy

Hour and buy two half-priced vanilla Dr. Peppers® (my drink of choice).

Jesus said:

> He who receives you receives me, and he who receives me receives the one who sent me. Anyone who receives a prophet because he is a prophet will receive a prophet's reward, and anyone who receives a righteous man because he is a righteous man will receive a righteous man's reward. And if anyone gives even a cup of cold water to one of these little ones because he is my disciple, I tell you the truth, he will certainly not lose his reward.
> —Matthew 10:40–42

Hospitality, especially when done for those the world deems insignificant, produces heavenly rewards. As you show hospitality to others, God will help you find your Jonathan.

FRIENDSHIP IN MARRIAGE

A major desire that couples have is for their partners to be a friend. In one study conducted with couples in all stages of the marriage relationship, couples were asked to rank a list of possible goals for their marriage. The single most important goal listed was to have a friend in one's partner.[3] In another study aimed at determining why singles wanted to get married, 84 percent described friendship as the primary reason. This should not be surprising, since the essence of marriage is to meet each other's need for companionship and to defeat loneliness. Researchers Notarius and Markman note that many couples said that in the process of divorce they "felt like they lost their best friend."[4] Work hard to keep friendship and fun in your marriage. In our marriage enrichment class we require date nights so that couples can begin again to do the things that attracted them to each other in the first place. A friend in a marriage partner is a great gift from God. Work to develop and nurture that friendship.

THE ONE TRUE FRIEND

Aristotle described friendship as "A single soul dwelling in two bodies." This type of friendship provides support, companionship, someone to be open and honest with, accountability, enjoyment in tasks done together, honest counsel, and protection. But as important as true biblical friendships are, there is still a great void in each heart that no human can ever fill. Even the truest companion cannot meet the deepest longing of your heart. That's a depth that can only be reached by God.

While the story of David and Jonathan provides great teaching about friendship, in reality it was short-lived. After a brief time of heartfelt companionship, David was on the run. Ten years later Jonathan was killed in battle.

David had other friends who hurt him deeply. In Psalm 41:9, David lamented, "Even my close friend, whom I trusted, he who shared my bread, has lifted up his heel against me." Later he felt the sting of another betrayal:

> If an enemy were insulting me, I could endure it; if a foe were raising himself against me, I could hide from him. But it is you, a man like myself, my companion, my close friend, with whom I once enjoyed sweet fellowship as we walked with the throng at the house of God.
>
> —Psalm 55:12–13

Human friendship can be fragile and fleeting. But there is One who will never leave us.

The deepest needs of David's heart were met by his Shepherd. He wrote about this relationship in what has become one of the most loved, memorized, and quoted passages in the Bible:

> The LORD is my shepherd; I have all that I need. He lets me rest in green meadows; he leads me beside peaceful streams. He renews my strength. He guides me along right paths, bringing honor to his name. Even when I walk through the darkest valley, I will not be afraid, for you are close beside me. Your rod and your staff protect and comfort me. You prepare a feast for me in the presence of my enemies. You honor me by anointing my head with oil. My cup overflows with blessings. Surely your goodness and unfailing love will pursue me all the days of my life, and I will live in the house of the LORD forever.
>
> —Psalm 23 (NLT)

Don't expect a friend to do what only God can do. The Great Shepherd loves you so much that he sent his Son to pay the penalty of your sins on the cross. Jesus is the only true friend who will never leave you or forsake you. A relationship with him is eternal. His love for you is unconditional. Jesus said:

> As the Father has loved me, so have I loved you. . . . Greater love has no one than this, that he lay down his life for his friends. You are my friends if you do what I command. I no longer call you servants, because a servant does not know his master's business. Instead, I have called you friends, for everything that I learned from my Father I have made known to you.
>
> —John 15:9–15

Invite God into your loneliness. He will meet you there and ignite your loneliness into a burning passion to follow hard after him.

Father, please give us true friends. Give us those who, like David and Jonathan, have the same passion to live for you. Give us friends who build us up and sharpen us for your sake.
Lord, reach to those who are lonely. Encourage their hearts. Remind them of your love.
Lead them to a spiritual community where life can be shared with one another.
Most of all, thank you for your friendship that never fades or fails. Ignite our hearts with a burning passion to always stay close to you.
In Jesus' name.
Amen.

Chapter 4

Igniting

a Stressed Heart

> *My body is resting every night, but my mind is spin-*
> *ning with all this [stuff]. It's hard to sleep. This is*
> *hard. I've never been through something like this. But*
> *when you get older, and have a bad year, you never*
> *know what can happen. A lot of times, they don't let*
> *you come back.*
>
> —David Ortiz
> Boston Red Sox Designated Hitter

David Ortiz was in a slump. The superstar Boston Red Sox designated hitter had a hard time making contact with the ball and getting on base. Ortiz has a lifetime batting average of .283 and for the last six seasons has averaged 39 home runs and 122 runs batted in. But this season was different. With the 2009 season almost 40 percent completed, Ortiz was batting .196 with two homers and 22 RBI's. His slump on the field impacted his entire life. Ortiz felt the stress.

> David Ortiz, who for six years was the life of the party in Boston, walks out of the shower and doesn't utter a word.

He reaches into his locker. Puts on his black Ed Hardy shirt and blue jeans. Fiddles with his iPod headset. And for the first time, looks around the Red Sox visiting clubhouse at the Detroit Tigers' Comerica Park.

He sees a gaggle of reporters around teammate Jason Bay, the left fielder. This is Ortiz's opening. He hurriedly shuffles past the crowd. Several reporters suddenly start to follow. If Ortiz notices he feigns ignorance.

Ortiz turns the corner and is out of sight. He retreats to the team hotel and heads to his room. He says he tried to sleep, but he couldn't. He shows up early the next day and sits slumped at his locker.

"My body is resting every night," he says, "but my mind is spinning with all this [stuff]. It's hard to sleep. This is hard. I've never been through something like this. But when you get older, and have a bad year, you never know what can happen. A lot of times, they don't let you come back."[1]

Have you ever buckled under the pressure? Has your spiritual average slipped? Been striking out a lot lately? Have you ever felt like you may be spiritually washed up? Does it feel like God has put you on the bench? Are you in a spiritual slump?

Don't despair. In this chapter we are going to follow David through an Ortiz-style slump and see how God got him back into his groove.

Man on the Run

David is the king-elect. He has been anointed by God, but the former king, Saul, has not accepted the new appointment.

Saul was mad with jealousy and made it his purpose in life to put the rookie to death. David is running for his life.

Always on the move, David, along with a few attendants, went to a little town called Nob. Ahimelech, the priest of Nob, was not all that pleased to see David. He asked "Why are you alone? Why is no one with you?" Ahimelech knew that Saul hated David. He knew David was a man on the run. And he also knew that any interaction with David would not be looked upon favorably by Saul. Scripture notes that Ahimelech was scared to death and "trembled" when he saw David coming (1 Sam. 21:1).

What happens next is so unlike David. The pressure is getting to him. The burden of running for his life day after day, month after month, year after year, had become so heavy that his emotional and spiritual legs begin to weaken and give out. Here is David's response to Ahimelech:

> David answered Ahimelech the priest, "The king charged me with a certain matter and said to me, 'No one is to know anything about your mission and your instructions.' As for my men, I have told them to meet me at a certain place. Now then, what do you have on hand? Give me five loaves of bread, or whatever you can find."
>
> —1 Samuel 21:2–3

Under pressure, David—the man after God's own heart— told an outright lie. He was not on a mission for the king; he was running from the king! He was not on the king's business; he *was* the king's business. Saul was hot on his trail. David was tired and hungry. He didn't have time to sit around and shoot the breeze. David looked Ahimelech right in the eyes and lied to get what he wanted.

STRESS AND SIN

Pressure, difficult situations, or fatigue don't always bring out the best in us, do they? When we are emotionally and physically worn out, we are vulnerable to sin. Temptation comes . . . every day. But when we are under stress the temptation to fall is greater.

In these tough economic times you need a certain quota for sales. The pressure is on. The temptation to make promises you can't keep and "play with" the numbers on the report are great.

You have to make a certain grade. The pressure is on. Everyone else cheats. It's not going to hurt this one time, is it?

I have never talked to anyone involved in an affair who said, "My marriage was tremendous. My husband and I got along splendidly. I walked right out of a happy home in the morning and got involved with someone in the afternoon." Most marriage wanderings are the result of long periods of stress in the relationship. I don't offer this as an excuse. There is no excuse for sin. But stressful situations make us vulnerable to temptation.

After David ate and prepared to leave, he asked the priest for a weapon. Listen as David continues the deception.

> David asked Ahimelech, "Don't you have a spear or a sword here? I haven't brought my sword or any other weapon, because the king's business was urgent." The priest replied, "The sword of Goliath the Philistine, whom you killed in the Valley of Elah, is here; it is wrapped in a cloth behind the ephod. If you want it, take it; there is no sword here but that one." David said, "There is none like it; give it to me."
>
> —1 Samuel 21:8–9

44

After David killed the giant Philistine, he took Goliath's sword, dedicated it to the Lord, and placed it in the tabernacle. God had graciously given David the victory, and as a sign of thankfulness he gave the sword back to God. Now with Saul in pursuit, David took back the sword he had once consecrated.

ANOTHER BAD DECISION

Under pressure David made another bad decision that led to compromise. With Saul right behind him, David headed for the Philistine city of Gath. One problem . . . Gath was the hometown of Goliath, and David, the man who had killed him, was carrying his sword. Perhaps David thought that his defeat of Goliath might give him some type of celebrity status. But that's not exactly what happened. When David arrived, the servants of Gath's King Achish said, "Isn't this David, the king of the land? Isn't he the one they sing about in their dances: 'Saul has slain his thousands, and David his tens of thousands'?" (1 Sam. 21:10–11). Here is David's response:

> David took these words to heart and was very much afraid of Achish king of Gath. So he pretended to be insane in their presence; and while he was in their hands he acted like a madman, making marks on the doors of the gate and letting saliva run down his beard.
>
> —1 Samuel 21:12–13

Amazing! This is David! The man after God's own heart! The anointed king of Israel! The giant killer under the stress of fear feigning insanity and acting like a madman! The king of Gath's response is classic. Seeing David with saliva running down his beard, he said, "Look at the man! He is insane! Why bring him to me? Am I so short of madmen that you have to bring this fellow here to carry on like this in front of me? Must this man come into my house?" (1 Sam. 21:14–15).

What was David thinking? Why did David feel the need to lie to Ahimelech the priest? Why would David go to the hometown of Goliath with the slain hero's sword? Why would the king of God's people pretend to be a madman? Let me take a shot at an answer. David was in the midst of a spiritual slump.

A SERIOUS SPIRITUAL SLUMP

I played baseball at a small college in Oklahoma. Our season stretched from the first of March to the end of May. We crammed a lot of games into that three-month period. And I had a few David Ortiz experiences. Some guys had slumps where in ten times at bat they failed to get a hit—they went 0 for 10. My slumps were different. Mine were like 0 for April! When you are in a serious slump one of the best things to do is sit out a game, take a seat on the bench, and regroup. That's what God did to David. David's bench was a cave.

David escaped from Gath and fled to the cave of Adullam. The king-elect—having lied to Ahimelech and feigned insanity before the Philistines—now hid in a damp, dark, cold cave.

Maybe you've been in a bit of a spiritual slump and you feel God has benched you. Perhaps you've made some bad decisions, you've buckled under pressure, or at a weak moment you gave into temptation. And God said, "Take a seat on the bench." You need to take some time to regroup. There are some important lessons to be learned while sitting out a game or two.

Lessons from the Bench

No player enjoys sitting on the bench. But God can and does use the time off the field to give us a better perspective of the game.

Getting Benched Can Produce Honesty

David has had a bad stretch—a spiritual slump. During this period he has lived light on the truth and heavy on deception. David's bench—the cave of Adullam—helped him get honest.

Psalm 142 is a prayer of David written "when he was in the cave." Listen to his honest conversation with God:

> I cry aloud to the Lord; I lift up my voice to the Lord for mercy. I pour out my complaint before him; before him I tell my trouble. When my spirit grows faint within me, it is you who know my way. In the path where I walk men have hidden a snare for me. Look to my right and see; no one is concerned for me. I have no refuge; no one cares for my life. I cry to you, O Lord; I say, "You are my refuge, my portion in the land of the living." Listen to my cry, for I am in desperate need; rescue me from those who pursue me, for they are too strong for me. Set me free from my prison, that I may praise your name. Then the righteous will gather about me because of your goodness to me.
>
> —Psalm 142:1–7

Being benched . . . in a cave . . . strips us of all pretenses, doesn't it? We admit our desperate need for God. We admit the challenges of life are too strong for us. We acknowledge that our "prison" is of our own making. There, in the cold and darkness, we realize that God is all we have . . . and is all we need. Just like David, we realize that God is our refuge. If you have been benched, pour your heart out to God. That may be why he has you there.

Getting Benched Can Bring Encouragement

In my personal baseball slumps and the benching that followed, I never had to sit alone for long. Another player would come and have a seat next to me. He would remind me of a slump he had and what he did to break out of it. The coach would walk by and tell me to keep my head up and that I'd be back in the lineup the next day. God does the same thing when we get benched in our spiritual slumps. He alone encourages the heart, and he often sends encouragement in human form.

When David's brothers and father heard about David's dilemma, they all went to visit him (1 Sam. 22:1). Think of David at his lowest, sitting alone on the bench. Then out of the blue he heard familiar voices. He heard his father and mother and brothers. David, now in his early twenties, ran to embrace his family. They hugged and kissed each other. Remember, David was the youngest of seven, so his brothers probably looked around the cave and said something like, "Hey, this is a pretty nice palace you have here . . . king." Then they laughed and assured him everything was going to be alright. When we cry out to God from our bench, he will send the encouragement just when we need it.

Getting Benched Can Prepare Us for the Future

God never wastes our time. He will even use our spiritual slumps for his game plan. While David was sitting on the bench in the cave, God sent him an army. Now, granted, this first army of David's was not a group of elite fighting men.

> All those who were in distress or in debt or discontented gathered around him, and he became their leader. About four hundred men were with him.
> —1 Samuel 22:2

God has a great sense of humor, doesn't he? David's first army was manned by men under stress—debtors who had given up trying to pay their bills, those who were discontented, men "in bitterness of soul"—because they had been wronged or mistreated. David probably kept Goliath's sword close by to protect himself from his own men!

David had to have thought, *Lord, what in the world are you doing? You need some help recruiting soldiers. Let me pick my own men next time.* But God was saying through this ragtag group, *David, always remember that I am your refuge and strength. You need soldiers, but always remember, I am the One who will fight your battles.*

David entered the cave alone and left as a leader. David took what God gave him and began to build and train an army. Some of these men became a special task force known as David's Mighty Men—the elite soldiers of their day. They remained loyal to David throughout their lives.

A Personal Cave

In March of 1977, my dad was diagnosed with cancer and given about six months to live. I was nineteen years old at the time. My mom, four older siblings, and I were all devastated by the news. As mentioned earlier, I played baseball at a small college and in the spring of 1977 learned that the college was going to discontinue the baseball program. My scholarship and social structure were gone and I began looking for another school where I could play. I had purchased a car about a year earlier and in May of that same year, I was caught in a flood.

The car was totaled and towed away. Then in August, my family gathered around my dad and watched him take his last breath and pass into the presence of his Savior.

With no place to play baseball and feeling like I should spend some time at home with my mom, I commuted to a local college during the fall semester. Each day I returned home to a house with my mom going through grief, missing my dad, missing my friends, and not knowing if I was going to ever find a place to play baseball. I felt God had benched me.

Like David, I cried out to God many times. I let him know I didn't appreciate what was going on in my life. He let me know how much he loved me. He brought encouragement in unlikely ways. And he used that benching to help prepare me for the rest of my life. That period of my life was cold, dark, and damp. But I wouldn't trade it for the world.

I have had some spiritual slumps since then, and I am sure there will be more in the future. But I have learned that God ignites a stressed heart . . . a benched heart . . . with encouragement and grace. God works mightily in the caves as we sit on the bench.

Father, I am certainly no fan of spiritual slumps and time sitting on the bench. But thank you for using all the challenges in my life to teach me lessons that I would have otherwise refused to hear. I pray for those who feel like you have placed them on the bench. Bring encouragement to their hearts. Get them back in the game.
For Christ's sake.
Amen.

Chapter 5

The LORD is close to the brokenhearted and saves those who are crushed in spirit.

—Psalm 34:18

Have you ever made a bad decision? How about a bad decision followed by a series of bad decisions? That's normally the way it happens, isn't it? Bad choices have a snowball effect. One usually leads to another. A sinful action followed by sinful cover-up followed by more disobedience. A hurtful remark responded to by an equally painful quip that ups the emotional ante and leads to resentment and disconnection (and more often than not some nasty gossip). An unguarded relationship that leads to an affair that leads to a divorce. A pile of broken hearts lies at the bottom of the downward spiral.

NOBODY WANTS A BROKEN HEART

No doubt, most people don't set out to make a mess of their lives. We dream great dreams. The thought of poor choices blowing up our dreams seldom crosses our mind.

In the premarital preparation that we require at our church, I instruct starry-eyed couples to write a marriage mission statement. I ask that they print the statements in their wedding programs and I work the mission into the ceremony. The statements are beautiful dreams of the future and commitments of loving each other and loving Christ. I have yet to see a statement that reads, "We really love each other now, but, after about five years, we plan to get a divorce and never deal with the issues that caused the demise of our marriage so that we can take those same issues into marriage number two and marriage number three. Our goal is to have strained relationships with our children, and we want our children's relationships with each other to be strained as well."

Nobody wants a broken heart. Nobody wants to be a heartbreaker. But it happens. Far too often it happens.

Discovering the Magical Formula

Maybe there is something a follower of Jesus can do to become immune to the plague of bad decisions and poor choices. Perhaps there is a series of Bible studies that provide guaranteed protection. Maybe on the twentieth anniversary of reading through the entire Bible, we finally and forever put to death the misdeeds of the body. Maybe memorizing a "life verse" is the key. Possibly the spiritual bulletproof vest is another book, seminar, conference, or really getting into the spiritual disciplines. Hey, here's one. What if God called you a person after his own heart? Surely, such a standing before God would protect you from making life-altering decisions and living with the consequences that follow, right? Not really.

TEN YEARS ON THE RUN

Normally, after a king is crowned, he moves into the palace and takes a seat on the throne. But the normal ascension to power was not God's plan for David. After telling David that he would be the next king of Israel, God took his time in telling Saul, the present king of Israel.

Saul developed a "jealous eye" for David. After a failed attempt to pin David to the palace wall with his spear, Saul chased David around the country like the FBI goes after the "most wanted." Saul pursued David for ten years! Think about how old you were and what you were doing ten years ago. Make a mental list of all the major experiences that have taken place in your life over the last decade. Now substitute all those experiences with this one—running for your life. David had been living like Harrison Ford in *The Fugitive* and was becoming a bit weary. He lived under the constant stress of survival. Fear hung over his head like that dirt cloud that always hovers over Linus in the *Peanuts* cartoons. And in that frame of mind, David made a really bad decision. He joined up with Israel's enemy. Listen to David's thought process:

> But David thought to himself, "One of these days I will be destroyed by the hand of Saul. The best thing I can do is to escape to the land of the Philistines. Then Saul will give up searching for me anywhere in Israel, and I will slip out of his hand."
> —1 Samuel 27:1

CLASSIC DECISION-MAKING MISTAKES

David made two classic mistakes in his decision-making process. First, he became his own counselor. David "thought to himself." He neglected to consult with God. The stressed-out, fearful fugitive determined that he was his best advisor. David didn't pray. He didn't seek counsel. His thinking was unilateral, and bad decisions are usually the result of one-sided thinking. That's certainly the way it works in my life. When I am stressed and not thinking clearly, I determine that I don't need to run my decision by God or anyone else. That's when I get into trouble. Those decisions have caused a lot of problems and taken a lot of work to correct. Solo decision-making is a surefire recipe for disaster—sooner or later.

The second flaw in David's decision-making process was this: he forgot God's promises. David convinced himself, "One of these days I will be destroyed at the hand of Saul." He had not heard that conclusion from God. The Lord had promised that David would lead the nation of Israel as king. But here David reaches his own conclusion. Ten years of running wears a person down. David was discouraged. Maybe God was not going to keep his promise after all. Maybe he had misunderstood. Whatever was going through David's worn-out mind, he made a bad decision. He crossed over to the enemy's side.

Don't Forget—Your Decisions Impact Others

Unfortunately, the consequences of an isolated decision aren't isolated. Your decision impacts others. In running from Saul, David had assembled a ragtag army of about six hundred men. These men, their wives, and their children traveled thirty miles on foot over rough terrain to the Philistine city of Gath. David's decision to join the enemy seemed to work. When Saul heard of David's escape to Gath "he no longer searched for him." Finally, some of the stress of running for his life was relieved.

The king of Gath directed David and his people to settle about twenty miles south of the city in a little village called Ziklag. They lived there for sixteen months. During that time, David made a living by raiding other countries.

> Now David and his men went up and raided the Geshurites, the Girzites and the Amalekites. (From ancient times these peoples had lived in the land extending to Shur and Egypt.) Whenever David attacked an area, he did not leave a man or woman alive, but took sheep and cattle, donkeys and camels, and clothes. Then he returned to Achish.
> —1 Samuel 27:8–9

It is important to note that the Geshurites, the Girzites, and the Amalekites were all enemies of Israel. But when Achish, one of the kings of Gath, asked for an accounting of the raids, David reported a list of Philistine enemies.

> When Achish asked, "Where did you go raiding today?" David would say, *"Against the Negev of Judah"* or *"Against the Negev of Jerahmeel"* or *"Against the Negev of the Kenites."* He did not leave a man or woman alive to be brought to Gath, for he thought, "They might inform on us and say, 'This is what David did.'" And such was his practice as long as he lived in Philistine territory.
> —1 Samuel 27:10–11, italics added

Think about what you have just read. For sixteen months David lived a life of compromise and deception. And one bad decision led to another.

When you live a life of lies you have to cover up your actions. David covered his tracks in an unthinkable and despicable way. Look again at the passage above. To make sure that no one informed on him, David "did not leave a man or woman alive" who might tell the real story. Deception is an insidious disease that eats away the core of our moral sensitivities.

The man after God's own heart, the servant of God, the anointed king of Israel, lived out his string of bad decisions one after another. Even Achish, the pagan Philistine king, concluded, "He has become so odious to his people, the Israelites, that he will be my servant forever" (1 Sam. 27:12).

Sometimes we read Scripture as a Bible storybook. All the cool stories are selected. We read our favorites like "The Shepherd Boy Anointed King" and "David Kills Goliath" as we tuck our children into bed. But Scripture is not to be viewed as stand-alone snapshots. An understanding of Scripture is like watching a video. When you read all the stories, you find that not every day in David's life was a giant-killing day. In fact, you find that on some of those non-giant-killing days, he made some really bad decisions followed by even more bad decisions which led to disastrous results. There's one thing we have to remember. All of our bad decisions, regardless of the frame of mind we were in when making them, carry consequences—as David was about to learn.

Five kings ruled the Philistine nation. Only one, King Achish, accepted and trusted David. When the Philistines gathered to battle with Israel, Achish was happy to have David and his men fight with him. But the other leaders said, "No way!" They were convinced that David would turn on them in the middle of the battle and start fighting for Israel. Achish reluctantly agreed and sent David and his men back home to Ziklag. That's when things went from bad to worse.

When David and his men returned to Ziklag, they came to a crest of a hill. Their homes were just over the hill. The weary soldiers envisioned their children playing outside and smoke coming from cooking fires. They could almost smell the aroma of their favorite foods. Their wives would see them and come running to jump into outstretched arms. They couldn't wait. But when they topped the hill their hearts sank. Anticipation turned to anguish. Their city was burned to the ground. The Amalekites, in retaliation of David's raiding parties, destroyed Ziklag and took the women and children captive. David and his brave fighting men "wept aloud until they had no strength left to weep" (1 Sam. 30:4). The tears came until the reservoir was dry. Then, the men blamed it all on David.

It was David's plan to join forces with the Philistines. He planned the raids against the Amalekites. In their pain and anger they determined that David was responsible. They made plans to stone him.

Can you imagine? What do you do when your heart is shattered, and you are the one holding the hammer that broke it into pieces? Here's what David finally did. He turned to God and asked that his burned-out heart be reignited. And when he did, "David found strength in the LORD his God" (1 Sam. 30:6). In the midst of his exhaustion, in the midst of his sin, in the midst of his discouragement, while his men were planning to pelt him to death with rocks, David turned to God and found everything that he needed.

WHOLENESS BRINGS CLARITY

Once David stopped depending on himself and turned to God, he started to think clearly. Faith replaced fear. Courage drove out confusion. Determination to do things correctly expelled deception and compromise. As a result, "David inquired of the LORD, 'Shall I pursue this raiding party? Will I overtake them?' 'Pursue them,' he answered. 'You will certainly overtake them and succeed in the rescue'" (1 Sam. 30:8). David and the Lord were communicating again. David was back on track.

WHOLENESS BRINGS RESOLVE

When God ignites your heart with strength, will you be ready to follow hard after him? David and his men, exhausted in body but strengthened in spirit, set out to claim God's promised victory. With the Lord's strength, everyone and everything the Amalekites took was recovered.

> David recovered everything the Amalekites had taken, including his two wives. Nothing was missing: young or old, boy or girl, plunder or anything else they had taken. David brought everything back.
>
> —1 Samuel 30:18–19

The strength that God gives will lead you to the process of recovery. There are going to be people from whom you need to ask forgiveness. There may be some difficult meetings where you confess your deception and compromise. It'll be difficult, but it'll be worth it in the end. And once you've received grace, it's time to extend it to others.

WHOLENESS SHARES GRACE

On the way to do battle with the Amalekites, David's army had to cross a ravine. Two hundred of David's men were so exhausted that they could not make the journey. David left them behind and moved ahead. Following the victory, David and the four hundred soldiers who made the rescue came to the place where the two hundred men were waiting.

> Then David came to the two hundred men who had been too exhausted to follow him and who were left

behind at the Besor Ravine. They came out to meet David and the people with him. As David and his men approached, he greeted them. But all the evil men and troublemakers among David's followers said, "Because they did not go out with us, we will not share with them the plunder we recovered. However, each man may take his wife and children and go."

David replied, "No, my brothers, you must not do that with what the LORD has given us. He has protected us and handed over to us the forces that came against us. Who will listen to what you say? The share of the man who stayed with the supplies is to be the same as that of him who went down to the battle. All will share alike."

—1 Samuel 30:21–24

When you think the battle was won by your skill and your intelligence and your strength, you, like the soldiers, will want to keep the plunder. But when you realize that all things come from God, you will share what he provides—especially grace. After the victory, David taught his soldiers a grace lesson. If the battle had depended on the strength of the fighting men, then certainly those too exhausted to participate should have received a smaller reward if any reward at all. But since David understood that God brought them victory and brought their wives and children back home, the outcome was clear: "The share of the man who stayed with the supplies is to be the same as that of him who went down to the battle. All will share alike."

David experienced grace; then he extended it. Maybe you need to do the same.

INVITE GOD INTO YOUR BROKENNESS

Are you living in brokenness? Are you there because of your bad decisions? Do you feel there is no way out? Good. Invite God to meet you there. Invite him into your broken, bleak, and seemingly irreversible situation. He can replace guilt with grace. He can give strength to your worn-out soul. He will give you the resolve to move on and recover the lost years, lost opportunities, even lost relationships. He replaces hopelessness with hope, confusion with clarity, and sadness with joy. God ignited David's brokenness with wholeness. He'll do the same for you.

> *The Lord is close to the brokenhearted and saves those who are crushed in spirit.*
> —Psalm 34:18

God ignites a heart with a burning passion to follow hard after him in the flames of brokenness . . .

> . . . when you are stripped and naked.
> . . . when your sin has been found out.
> . . . when you ache with shame.
> . . . when the consequences seem overwhelming.
> . . . when forgiveness seems uncertain.

God is close to the brokenhearted. Reach out and take his hand.

God ignites a heart with a burning passion to follow hard after him in the flames of brokenness . . .

> . . . when the loss is unbearable.
> . . . when the waves of grief hit hard.
> . . . when the pain is paralyzing.

   . . . when you miss them.
   . . . on their birthday.
   . . . on your anniversary.
   . . . at Christmas.

God is close to the brokenhearted. Reach out and take his hand.

God ignites a heart with a burning passion to follow hard after him in the flames of brokenness . . .

   . . . when unfaithfulness is discovered.
   . . . when there is no intention to break it off.
   . . . when you can't control the tears.
   . . . when just getting out of bed in the morning is a chore.
   . . . when you have to tell your friends.
   . . . when you have to tell the kids.
   . . . when you see him with the other woman.
   . . . when she looks so happy with the other man.
   . . . when you can't describe how bad it hurts.

God is close to the brokenhearted. Reach out and take his hand.

God ignites a heart with a burning passion to follow hard after him in the fires of brokenness . . .

   . . . when the results show cancer.
   . . . when the cancer shows up again.
   . . . when you are wheeled into surgery.
   . . . when the doctors come to tell you how the surgery went.
   . . . when the chemo starts.
   . . . when the nausea comes.

. . . when your hair starts falling out.

. . . when the nights are long.

God is close to the brokenhearted. Reach out and take his hand.

> *Father, some reading this are broken. Please meet them*
> *right where they are. Wrap your arms around them.*
> *Offer them forgiveness. Bring wholeness into their lives.*
> *By your grace restore what was lost. Ignite their broken*
> *hearts with a burning passion to follow hard after you.*
> *Reach out and take their hands.*
> *In Christ's name.*
> *Amen.*

Chapter 6

Igniting a Heart on Hold

> *We wait in hope for the LORD; he is our help and our shield. In him our hearts rejoice, for we trust in his holy name.*
>
> —Psalm 33:20–21

The flight was brutal. I had never made a long transatlantic flight on such a small plane. Our departure was delayed for an hour as we waited in the stuffy, crowded aircraft while the pilot calibrated headwinds and fuel capacity. Before taxiing to the runway, he informed us that the flight would not be nonstop to New York as originally planned. We would land somewhere in Canada to refuel.

On the other side of the aisle sat six or seven rambunctious—no, that's too kind—obnoxious teenagers. Seated in the front and back of an older couple, they made the man and woman's life miserable for several hours. Kind requests to settle down, not-so-kind requests from the people around them, and stern lectures from the flight attendants did little more than provide a short breather from their boorishness.

Finally, at the end of the exhausting ordeal, we began our final descent into JFK. But as we hovered over New York City, the captain's voice came over the intercom informing us that the current air traffic had forced us into a holding pattern. I hate holding patterns. And I hated the next forty-five minutes. My head was throbbing as we circled and circled and then did a few figure eights just for fun. Thankfully, we had stopped in Canada to refuel because we were going to need it.

I don't like traffic jams on the ground, but I definitely didn't enjoy the feeling that the plane was coming to a stop five thousand feet in the air. And those banking turns? Way too steep for my stomach. My head really began to ache. I closed my eyes to endure the torture. I don't like holding patterns in planes, and I am not fond of holding patterns in life.

Have you ever felt like God has put you in a holding pattern? Have you yearned for something to happen? You prayed hard and often, and then you waited . . . and waited . . . and waited? After a while your prayerful desire turned to deep disappointment. After a while your dreams began to mock you.

What do you do? Where do you turn? Let's continue to follow David, the man after God's own heart, to learn how to deal with the tough process of waiting.

GET OUT THE WHITE FLAG

When David was a fifteen-year-old shepherd, the prophet Samuel found him in the fields, whispered in his ear, "You are the next king of Israel," and then poured anointing oil on his head. For the next five years David knew nothing but success. There was the big win over Goliath. The newcomer led military campaigns to significant victories. Songs were written about David and sung by the young maidens throughout the land.

Someone has said that the most dangerous thing a person can experience is too much success too early in life. Perhaps that's why, after five years of David's wooing the hearts of Israel, God placed David in a holding pattern. Saul, who still thought that he was king, grew insane with jealousy and chased David around the countryside for the next ten years. And during his personal holding pattern David experienced a tenderizing process of waiting.

Some of you are on hold as you read these words. You know all about the emotions in the waiting room of life. How do you continue to believe that God answers prayer when your request goes unanswered for a month? A year? Five years? A decade? Or even longer? Think about what David must have felt.

David was no Eleanor Rigby. He didn't have a stash of masks. When he talked to God, he expressed his heart. Listen to the emotions pouring out of David's heart in Psalm 13:

> How long, O LORD? Will you forget me forever?
> How long will you hide your face from me? How
> long must I wrestle with my thoughts and every day
> have sorrow in my heart? How long will my enemy
> triumph over me?
>
> —Psalm 13:1–2

Have you ever asked these questions: Lord, have you forgotten me? Are you hiding from me? I was minding my own business. I was taking care of sheep, and you sent Samuel to find me. Why did you call me to *this*? Why did you put this *desire* in my heart, give me a *taste* of fulfilled promises, and then put me on the run? How long will I have to wait?

Keep reading Psalm 13 and you'll see that Saul was gaining ground on David.

> Look on me and answer, O LORD my God. Give
> light to my eyes, or I will sleep in death; my enemy
> will say, "I have overcome him," and my foes will
> rejoice when I fall.
>
> —Psalm 13:3–4

David called on God to answer his prayer. You can, too. God knows what's on your mind. He understands your frustrations. He can handle your inquiries. Don't think that you might surprise him with your emotions. Talk to your heavenly Father about everything that is on your heart.

David wrote this psalm after the events that brought on these emotions. We don't know how long he languished in such a difficult emotional state as recorded in the first four verses. It could have been days, months, or even years. What we do know is that at some point David made a decision. Nothing seems to have changed in his surroundings, but he came to a conclusion. I imagine David going through all the intent and urgent emotions of the first verses and then before the last two verses, heaving a big sigh and proclaiming, "But I trust in your unfailing love; my heart rejoices in your salvation. I will sing to the LORD, for he has been good to me" (Ps. 13:5–6).

Do you see what David did in these last verses? He surrendered. In essence, he says, "Lord, it seems that you have forgotten me. It seems that you are hiding from me. I have been on the run for a long time. You made promises to me. Where are your provisions?" And then, with a big sigh, he says, "Okay, I surrender. You win. You are God; I am not. I trust in your unfailing love."

God's "unfailing love" comes from the Hebrew word *hesed*. It explains not only a deep emotion but a deep commitment. It describes a loyal, nonnegotiable love that God has for all who trust him. This psalm begins with David's emotional questioning. It ends with a settled trust in the loyal love of the heavenly Father. Commenting on the variation of emotion expressed in David's words, C. H. Spurgeon emphasizes the contrast.

> What a change is here! Lo, the rain is over and gone, and the time of the singing of birds is come. The mercy-seat has so refreshed the poor weeper, that he clears his throat for a song. If we have mourned with him, let us now dance with him. David's heart was more often out of tune than his harp. He begins many of his Psalms sighing, and ends them singing . . . . It is worthy to be observed that the joy is all the greater because of the previous sorrow, as calm is all the more delightful in recollection of the preceding tempest.[1]

God ignites our heart when we finally say, "You win! You've got me! Take away my desires and longings and turn my heart wholly and fully to you. Break down the walls and let the blaze spread. I trust in your unfailing love."

But let's face it. Words are easy; action is hard. It's one thing to say, "God, you win." It's another thing to give up "my rights." We must move from declaration to acceptance. "Lord, not only do I declare you the winner, I am willing to trust you with my present circumstances. I am willing to accept this holding pattern, and I'll stay in it until you give me the clearance to land." Let's see how David worked through the surrender process.

"HOW THE MIGHTY HAVE FALLEN!"

In the first chapter of 2 Samuel, David learned that Saul and his son Jonathan had been killed in battle. The messenger who brought the news held Saul's crown. A decade of running was over. Finally, the crown was officially his. Time to party! Uncork the bottles! Not so fast.

When David heard the news, he wept and mourned the loss of Jonathan. You would expect that. He and Jonathan were kindred spirits. But he also mourned the death of the man who tried to pin him to the wall with a spear and chased him around the countryside with the expressed intent of ending his life. David wrote a lament for both Saul and his son Jonathan. David ordered all his men to learn it. Read the lament and note the honor that David gave these slain leaders.

> Your glory, O Israel, lies slain on your heights. How the mighty have fallen! Tell it not in Gath, proclaim it not in the streets of Ashkelon, lest the daughters of the Philistines be glad, lest the daughters of the uncircumcised rejoice. O mountains of Gilboa, may you have neither dew nor rain, nor fields that yield offerings of grain. For there the shield of the mighty was defiled, the shield of Saul—no longer rubbed with oil. From the blood of the slain, from the flesh of the mighty, the bow of Jonathan did not turn back, the sword of Saul did not return unsatisfied. Saul and Jonathan—in life they were loved and gracious, and in death they were not parted. They were swifter than eagles, they were stronger than lions. O daughters of Israel, weep for Saul, who clothed you in scarlet and finery, who adorned your garments with ornaments of gold. How the mighty have fallen in battle! Jonathan lies slain on your heights. I grieve for you, Jonathan my brother; you were very dear to me. Your love for me was wonderful, more wonderful than that of women. How the mighty have fallen! The weapons of war have perished!
>
> —2 Samuel 1:19–27

What a beautiful eulogy. He reminded the people of Saul's leadership. He reminded the people that Saul had provided well for them. Under his kingship they had been clothed with "scarlet and finery," adorned with "ornaments of gold." David wrote this for the one who had made his life a nightmare for an entire decade! Could you do that? *Can* you do that?

Remember, surrendering is a process. And at some point in that process you have to accept that which caused the pain. A surrendered heart comes to an understanding of God's sovereign work in our life. Even though we don't understand the "whys," God really does work out all things for "the good of those who love him, who have been called according to his purpose" (Rom. 8:28).

THE WAITING IS OVER! KIND OF . . .

The prophet Samuel had anointed David in a private ceremony fifteen years earlier. Now the anointing was public. After all the years of running, David was finally the king, but the waiting was not over.

David was anointed king over a divided country. The northern kingdom was called Israel and the southern kingdom, Judah. When David was crowned king of Judah, another coronation was taking place in Israel. Abner, the commander of Saul's army, took it upon himself to name a successor for his fallen leader. He chose one of Saul's sons, Ish-Bosheth, and named him king. These kingdoms engaged in a civil war that lasted for the next seven-and-a-half years. The hatred grew between the north and south. And David waited for God's promise—that he would be king over the entire nation—to be fully realized. It took some time, but his surrendered heart finally paid off.

Abner was the commander of the Israelite army, and Joab led David's army. The two sides met for battle at the pool of

Gibeon, and that day Joab was victorious. After the defeat, Abner and his men headed for the hills and Joab's men gave chase. Joab's brother, Asahel, pursued Abner. The good news was that Asahel was fast, "as fleet-footed as a wild gazelle." But that was also bad news for Asahel. Abner looked back and saw his predicament. He warned Asahel to stop. But the fleet-footed young man kept closing the gap. When Asahel caught up, Abner took the butt of his spear and thrust it into Asahel's stomach. The collision of the spear going one direction and Asahel going the other did severe damage. Asahel died on the spot. With the death of his brother, Joab's hatred for Abner and the northern kingdom became very personal.

The battles continued over the years. David's army grew stronger; Ish-Bosheth's troops grew weaker. David could have taken matters into his own hands and defeated the northern army. But his heart was surrendered to God. So, David waited and waited. In due time, God caused the northern kingdom to implode.

In the midst of the civil war, an internal conflict arose in the north when Ish-Bosheth accused Abner of sleeping with one of Saul's former concubines. In that day, such an action was not simply a moral issue. If true, it demonstrated that Abner was assuming Saul's authority.

Abner went ballistic. He not only denied the charge but turned on Ish-Bosheth. He made arrangements to meet with David and promised to bring the northern army to David's side. That was good news until Joab got wind of the plan. He wanted no part of an alliance with the man who had killed his brother. Joab arranged a secret meeting with Abner under the guise of friendship. But when the two were alone, Joab took his personal revenge. And the killing continued.

When Ish-Bosheth son of Saul heard that Abner had died in Hebron, he lost courage, and all Israel became alarmed. Now Saul's son had two men who were leaders of raiding bands. One was named Baanah and the other Recab. . . . Now Recab and Baanah, the sons of Rimmon the Beerothite, set out for the house of Ish-Bosheth, and they arrived there in the heat of the day while he was taking his noonday rest. They went into the inner part of the house as if to get some wheat, and they stabbed him in the stomach. Then Recab and his brother Baanah slipped away. They had gone into the house while he was lying on the bed in his bedroom. After they stabbed and killed him, they cut off his head.

—2 Samuel 4:1–2a; 5–7

The Israelites—the northern kingdom—lost their king and commander. They came to David desiring that the kingdoms be united. Here's the account:

All the tribes of Israel came to David at Hebron and said, "We are your own flesh and blood. In the past, while Saul was king over us, you were the one who led Israel on their military campaigns. And the Lord said to you, 'You will shepherd my people Israel, and you will become their ruler.'" When all the elders of Israel had come to King David at Hebron, the king made a compact with them at Hebron before the Lord, and they anointed David king over Israel. David was thirty years old when he became king, and he reigned forty years. In Hebron he reigned over Judah seven years and six months, and in Jerusalem he reigned over all Israel and Judah thirty-three years.

—2 Samuel 5:1–5

KING OF ISRAEL! FINALLY!

This was the third time David was anointed king. The first time, he was a fifteen-year-old shepherd boy. After five years of success and a decade of running, he was anointed king over half of the kingdom. Then, after another seven-and-a-half years, David became king of a united Israel. David endured twenty-two years of waiting and waiting and waiting.

Now here's the question: Was there a purpose to all the waiting? How did God use this period of waiting in David's life? Let's see what lessons we can learn.

Waiting on God Produces Dependence on God

The only thing that stood between David and the crown was Saul. Now Saul was dead. The messenger who brought the news brought Saul's crown with him. I am certain that after all those years of waiting, many of us would have had the crown on our head. Not David. David's holding pattern had taught him not to take matters into his own hands. The first thing he did was to seek God's direction.

> In the course of time, David inquired of the LORD. "Shall I go up to one of the towns of Judah?" he asked. The LORD said, "Go up." David asked, "Where shall I go?" "To Hebron," the LORD answered. So David went up there with his two wives, Ahinoam of Jezreel and Abigail, the widow of Nabal of Carmel. David also took the men who were with him, each with his family, and they settled in Hebron and its towns. Then the men of Judah came to Hebron and there they anointed David king over the house of Judah.
>
> —2 Samuel 2:1–4

Like every new king, David was tested by his enemies. When the Philistines heard that David was king over all of Israel they determined to make his reign a short one. They "went up in full force to search for him" (2 Sam. 5:17). So David, a man trained in the holding pattern, asked the Lord, "Shall I go and attack the Philistines? Will you hand them over to me?" The Lord answered him, "Go, for I will surely hand the Philistines over to you" (2 Sam. 5:19).

The prophet Isaiah said that God "acts on behalf of those who wait on him" (Isa. 64:4). David had learned that lesson in the igniting process of waiting. How about you? Will you demonstrate your dependence on God by waiting for him to act on your behalf? How many things in our lives have we messed up by taking matters into our own hands? Are you willing to wait on God?

Waiting on God Produces Patience

Many of you will be able to relate to a *Calvin and Hobbes* cartoon I recently read.

Frame 1: The setting is late November and Calvin is waiting by his sled for the first big snowfall. He waits and waits and waits but no snow.

Frame 2: Calvin says, "If I were in charge, we'd never see grass between October and May." Then looking to the heavens he says, "On three. Ready? One . . . Two . . . Three . . . Snow!" But nothing happens.

Frame 3: Calvin shouts to the heavens, "I said snow, c'mon— snow!" Shaking his fist to the heavens he shouts, "Snow!"

Frame 4: Disgusted with God's failure to deliver, he says, "OK, then, don't snow! See if I care! I like this weather. Let's have it forever!" But his defiance is short-lived.

Frame 5: Calvin is on his knees, praying, "Please snow! Please? Just a foot! Or eight inches! That's all! Six inches, even! How about just six?" The he looks to the heavens and shouts, "I'm waaiiting!"

Frame 6: Calvin is running in a circle, head down, fists clenched. All he can say is "RRRRGGHH!"

Frame 7: Calvin is exhausted. His energy is spent. His prayer is unanswered. He looks up to God and cries out in desperation: "Do you want ME to become an ATHEIST?"

Is patience just a personality thing? Is it something in our genes? Is patience something we can learn?

In Psalm 40, David likened the holding pattern to being in a "slimy pit," stuck in the "mud and mire." But that's where David learned, and where we can learn, the benefits to waiting on God.

> I waited patiently for the LORD; he turned to me and heard my cry. He lifted me out of the slimy pit, out of the mud and mire; he set my feet on a rock and gave me a firm place to stand. He put a new song in my mouth, a hymn of praise to our God. Many will see and fear and put their trust in the LORD.
>
> —Psalm 40:1–3

Can you relate to the feeling of being stuck in the "mud and mire"? Movement is slow. Every step takes great effort. Your footing is unsure. In the "slimy pit" there is uncertainty and unsteadiness. Been there? Maybe you are there now. Let's learn from David's experience.

First, cry out to God. David lived unmasked before his Father. He needed help and wasn't afraid to ask for it. He was not ashamed to admit that he didn't like the holding pattern, that walking in the "mud and mire" was not his strong suit. He was in a deep hole and not too proud to cry out to the only One who could remedy his slimy situation. Why do so many of us think that somehow we can lift ourselves out of our pits? Like David, cry out to God.

Second, here's the hard part. Pray for patience. It is a fruit of the Spirit. Don't expect God to deliver you in the next nanosecond. He will keep you in the holding pattern until you have learned all you need to learn. So wait patiently and listen to the Teacher.

Third, praise God. Too many believers quickly forget what God has done. Having been lifted from the pit and placed on the rock, we simply clean off the mud and resume the fast pace in our preferred direction. Sometimes we downplay the whole pit experience. "It wasn't that bad after all. I just panicked a bit. I could have gotten out on my own. I could have climbed my way to the rock." Why do we do that? How about some praise! How about acknowledging the Deliverer! How about shouting the new song he has put in our mouths.

Finally, tell others. What God does for us will be a great encouragement to those on hold. Slimy-pit deliverances should be community celebrations. Let the church know what God has done so the community can rejoice and worship together.

Waiting on God Produces Trust

God will work things out in his own way in his own time. David learned this time and time again. His waiting on God produced a deep trust in God. Time and time again God delivered. That's why the psalmist can say, "We wait in hope for the LORD; he is our help and shield. In him our hearts rejoice, for we trust in his holy name" (Ps. 33:20–21).

Isaiah the prophet adds this commitment from his personal heart-on-hold experience. Even when God was "hiding his face," Isaiah said, "I will wait for the LORD, who is hiding his face from the house of Jacob, I will put my trust in him" (Isa. 8:17).

We want God to work in our lives now. Like Calvin, we are "waaiiting!" But the stories of Scripture and the stories of Christian history remind us that many times God's people are put in a holding pattern. We are called to trust even though we may never see that for which we have waited.

In his book *Loving God*, Charles Colson gives this account of some mighty men of God who prayed and waited but never saw the fruit of their prayers:

> The great colonial pastor Cotton Mather prayed for revival several hours each day for twenty years; the Great Awakening began the year he died. The British Empire finally abolished slavery as the Christian parliamentarian and abolitionist William Wilberforce lay on his deathbed, exhausted from his nearly fifty-year campaign against the practice of human bondage. Few were the converts during Hudson Taylor's lifelong mission work in the Orient: but today millions of Chinese embrace the faith he so patiently planted and tended.
>
> Some might think this divine pattern cruel, but I am convinced there is a sovereign wisdom to it. Knowing how susceptible we are to success's siren call, God does not allow us to see, and therefore glory in, what is done through us. The very nature of obedience He demands is that it be given without regard to circumstances or results.[2]

You see, God calls us to wait . . . and trust him for the results in his timing and in his way. Invite God into your holding pattern. He will teach you patience. Ask him to help you learn the lessons he has for you. And remember, God works on one timetable—his.

God's Schedule Is Not Always Our Schedule

God likes to remind me that I'm on his schedule, not my own. Several years ago, my wife, Lori, and I had everything planned out. We would get married, go to seminary, and then get involved in church ministry. Pastor, associate pastor, pastor of whatever, it didn't matter. I had felt called into the ministry for as long as I could remember. Lori and I couldn't wait. But some things happened that forced us to put seminary on hold for a year after we were married. It was a small bump in our plans. But the year passed quickly and we headed to Dallas.

Lori worked as an accountant for what was then one of the Big Eight accounting firms. I focused on classes and worked during the summer. A three-month internship overseas and preaching each Sunday at a little church during my last year whetted our appetites even more. Finally, graduation came, but church opportunities did not. So I waited. During my seminary years I painted houses for a man who owned rental property around the Dallas area. After my graduation, with no church leads, and still painting houses, he chuckled, "Well, I guess God needs painters more than preachers." I smiled, but inside I wondered if that might be true for me. And I felt pretty low.

At the end of the summer, I found out about a teaching and coaching position at Sunnyvale Independent School District, just outside of Dallas. My undergraduate degree was in education, and I had taught and coached for a year after college.

They were desperate and so was I. "I'll only be doing this for a semester, maybe a year," I reasoned. But God's plans were different. I stayed at Sunnyvale for the next four-and-a-half years.

For the first two years I really struggled. Why did God put this longing in my heart for ministry in a church? Why had I invested four years in seminary? What was wrong with me that God wasn't providing an opportunity? I let God know I didn't approve of what he was doing. I let him know often that I didn't appreciate having my heart locked into a holding pattern.

About the same time that I started teaching at Sunnyvale, a part-time opportunity with a start-up church in Atlanta, Texas, arose. Lori and I decided to give it a shot. We would leave for Atlanta on Friday evening and spend the weekend in a rented house that served as our living quarters and the meeting place for the church on Sundays. At the time, Lori was pregnant with our first child. Five hours in the car and staying in that house each weekend was tough, especially for her. The church invited us to move to Atlanta in an attempt to build the church.

I called a former seminary professor for advice. He said, "If you really want to make it work, the day that you arrive there, go to the cemetery and pick out a plot. That's the type of commitment it will take." That was hard to hear. I'm from Oklahoma. Living in Texas was bad enough, but being buried there was unthinkable! We decided not to make the move. One of the elders at the church told me I was making the biggest mistake of my life. My dream was starting to disappear.

But still I waited.

After about two years of struggling with God, I surrendered. I raised the white flag. By this time, Lori and I had a daughter and another child on the way. I had the opportunity to work in Sunnyvale's administration. I started working on a master's degree in educational administration. We bought a house and sank some money into fixing it up. I surrendered. I would be buried in Texas after all.

That's when I discovered that there are two parts to the surrendering process. After two years at Sunnyvale, I made my declaration: "God, you win! I give up. I hope you're happy, because I'm not!" God wasn't thrilled with my attitude so he gave me some more time to deal with it. Two years after I said "You win!" I finally said, "I accept. You are God; I am not."

After four-and-a-half years, God presented us with a church opportunity in Pennsylvania. After the initial church interview I told Lori, "If they call and say thanks but no thanks, that will be fine with me." But again, God had a different plan. The invitation came. We accepted and have been at the same church for twenty years.

Waiting is not a waste of time in God's economy. He uses it to prepare us for the next assignment. Without the spiritual stretching and practical skills acquired during my time at Sunnyvale, I would have never lasted in ministry. Or had I lasted, I would have made a mess of a few churches along the way.

But my waiting wasn't all about preparation for my next assignment. Just as I was waiting on God, he was waiting on me. I had written my own plans that just happened to include him. He wanted me to follow his plans, ignited by him. A. W. Tozer said that God "waits to be wanted. Too bad that with many of us he waits so long, so very long, in vain."[3]

God taught me those lessons about waiting many years ago and you might think that I have never struggled with waiting since, but that's not the case. You'd think four-and-a-half years at Sunnyvale would have gotten the point across, but it seems God always has some dream, some desire, some part of my heart on hold, waiting on me to go through the process so that he can use my surrendered heart.

I know that my story may be minor league compared to yours. You might be in a holding pattern that has lasted much longer, but the principle is still the same. When we surrender to God and come to terms with being surrendered, he does marvelous things. I don't know what God has in store for you, but I do know that when you surrender your heart, he will ignite it with a burning passion to follow hard after him. That's what he has wanted all along.

Surrender your heart on hold to God. He will ignite it . . . even while you wait.

> *Father, I pray for all those who feel like their lives are in a holding pattern. Maybe they are single and desiring to find a mate. Maybe their career has stalled. Maybe a dream continues to remain a dream. Maybe they feel that there is something you want them to do but they can't get clarity. Maybe they have clarity but someone or something is holding them back. Lord, ignite the hearts of those on hold with a burning passion to fully submit themselves to you. Use their burning heart for your eternal purpose.*
> *I pray in Christ's name.*
> *Amen.*

Chapter 7

LORD JESUS,
I am blind, be thou my light,
ignorant, be thou my wisdom,
self-willed, be thou my mind.
                    —*The Valley of Vision*

Let's try a little exercise. See the plus sign and dot below?
Cover your left eye, and look at the plus sign with your
right eye. Don't look at the circle; you will be able to see it in
your peripheral vision. Now, hold the book a foot away from
your face and begin to move it closer to your face.

At some point you will not be able to see the circle. That
point is your blind spot and every person has one. At a certain
point, in a certain position, there are some things you cannot

81

see. The object doesn't disappear; it simply moves out of your sight.

WE ALL HAVE BLIND SPOTS—EVEN SPIRITUAL ONES

Would you agree with me that just as physical blind spots exist, so do spiritual ones? Would you agree that it's possible for believers—even strong believers—to be completely blind to an important issue in their life? Let me offer some examples.

How about Christians who are committed to a daily quiet time but have never given close to a tithe? Reading God's Word on a regular basis is an essential spiritual discipline. But responding to what God's Word says about money and giving is just as critical. Daily devotions without generosity of resources? That's a blind spot.

How about believers who are applauded for their service in the church while neglecting their responsibilities at home? Loving your wife as Christ loved the church and spending time with your children to teach them and show them the characteristics of a Christ-follower is the calling of every husband and father. Serving the church without serving your family? That's a blind spot.

Here's one more. This is one of my favorites. Years ago an individual chided my wife for not purchasing her wardrobe at a local discount store. She lectured my wife on the issue of stewardship. Certainly, in principle she was right. We should always demonstrate good stewardship in our purchasing. But there was this one little thing our well-meaning friend missed. She left the discount store parking lot in her posh little sports car and pulled into the driveway of her large, expensive home. She pounded the pulpit about clothes shopping but didn't quite apply the same principle elsewhere. When Lori came home that day and told me this story, I hopped into my twelve-year-old Honda, drove to her house, and let her have it! Just kidding.

I have my share of blind spots. You do too. Your blind spot might be a particular character flaw. It's visible to others, but not to you. Maybe your blind spot is a particular attitude toward someone or something. Others see it as clearly as the nose on your face. You look in the mirror every day and flat miss it. Maybe your blind spot is the neglect of a certain spiritual discipline. Your interpretation of "prayer and fasting" is "pray fast." Pesky little things, those blind spots.

I vividly remember one of my seminary professors telling a story about the school's earlier years. He said that for the first forty years or so African-American students were not admitted. Then he asked with a frown, "Can you believe we did that? That was wrong. We have no excuse for such a negligence and sin. We were blinded." Then he posed a second question: "What are we missing today that when we look back on thirty years from now people will ask, 'What were they thinking?' We know what our blind spot *was*, but what *is* our blind spot today?" Great question, isn't it? What is your blind spot today?

DAVID AND HIS SERIOUS BLIND SPOTS

David was not immune to blind spots, even some glaring ones. But God has a way of opening our eyes. He ignites the blinded heart with a wake-up call. After a decade of running from the jealous Saul, David began to see God's promise come true. David won an impressive battle to capture the strongly fortified city of Jerusalem. He devised a clever plan to make his way into the middle of the city by way of an underground water tunnel. He surprised the enemy and took over the city. He headquartered his army in Jerusalem, and it became known as the "City of David."

David was living in a stretch of successes. He was strategizing brilliant battle plans. He was leading his men on the battlefield. He was a strong and victorious leader. Israel was enjoying great blessing. Like a luscious fruit that explodes with flavor and delights the taste buds, so success explodes with satisfaction and delights the heart. David tasted the sweet fruit of achievement and accomplishment. He became more and more powerful, "because the LORD God Almighty was with him" (2 Sam. 5:10).

One of the reasons I love Scripture is because God's inspired Word tells it like it is. Nothing is sugar-coated or covered up. While this great leader, this man after God's own heart, was experiencing great success, Scripture records some of David's serious blind spots. Let's start with his family.

> Sons were born to David in Hebron: His firstborn was Amnon . . . his second, Kileab . . . the third, Absalom . . . the fourth, Adonijah . . . the fifth, Shephatiah . . . and the sixth, Ithream . . . These were born to David in Hebron.
>
> —2 Samuel 3:2–5

Six sons! What a great blessing! Oh, you know what? I left out some important information.

> Sons were born to David in Hebron: His firstborn was Amnon the son of Ahinoam of Jezreel; his second, Kileab the son of Abigail the widow of Nabal of Carmel; the third, Absalom the son of Maacah daughter of Talmai king of Geshur; the fourth, Adonijah the son of Haggith; the fifth, Shephatiah the son of Abital; and the sixth, Ithream the son of David's wife Eglah. These were born to David in Hebron.
>
> —2 Samuel 3:2–5

During David's seven-and-a-half years in Hebron, he had six wives. David, I think we see a blind spot. The writer makes no criticism or judgment here. The facts are simply stated. Instead, he let the tragic results of David's blind spot speak for themselves. And then David's blind spot gets bigger.

> After he left Hebron, David took more concubines and wives in Jerusalem, and more sons and daughters were born to him. These are the names of the children born to him there: Shammua, Shobab, Nathan, Solomon, Ibhar, Elishua, Nepheg, Japhia, Elishama, Eliada and Eliphelet.
>
> —2 Samuel 5:13–16

"Well, come on," I hear you saying, "That's not a blind spot. It's the Old Testament. Everyone was doing it." By the way, that's the classic rationale for blind spots—everybody's doing it. I remember my oldest daughter saying, "Dad, there's this sleepover, and it's co-ed. But the boys will be *way down* in the basement and girls will be *way up* on the second floor. Before you say no, everybody's going to be there." I simply sighed and said, "Sweetie, sweetie, sweetie, the statement you made is incorrect. Everybody won't be there because *you* won't be there."

Many multi-marriages were taking place in the OT, but that didn't make them right. Let's go back and check God's idea for marriage.

> But for Adam no suitable helper was found. So the LORD God caused the man to fall into a deep sleep; and while he was sleeping, he took one of the man's ribs and closed up the place with flesh. Then the LORD God made a woman from the rib he had taken out of the man, and he brought her to the man. The man said, "This is now bone of my bones

> and flesh of my flesh; she shall be called 'woman,'
> for she was taken out of man." For this reason a
> man will leave his father and mother and be united
> to his wife, and they will become one flesh.
>
> —Genesis 2:20b–24

For David's sake, I'm looking for loopholes. "No suitable helper." Hmm, that's singular isn't it? "United to his wife." Not wives? "And they will become one flesh." Not one flesh at a time, just one flesh. God's plan and design has always been one man, one woman, for life.

Well, maybe there was a royal exception for the one wife thing. Certainly kings wanted a lot of children to keep the royal bloodlines flowing. Maybe, more than one wife was a kingly privilege? Perhaps we can find a "royal exception clause." Let's check the Mosaic Law.

> When you enter the land the LORD your God is giv-
> ing you and have taken possession of it and settled
> in it, and you say, "Let us set a king over us like
> all the nations around us," be sure to appoint over
> you the king the LORD your God chooses. . . . He
> must not take many wives, or his heart will be led
> astray.
>
> —Deuteronomy 17:14–17

Only six generations existed from Adam before polygamy entered the scene. It was never God's plan. Due to the hardness of hearts (blind spots), God allowed it. But sin always carries consequences. Don't think for one minute that your heavenly Father, who loves you so much that he sent his Son to die for your sin, will let you skip merrily through life with spiritual blind spots. Sooner or later, God will send a wake-up call. And if you ignore the call, things may get a lot worse before they get better.

DON'T EVER THINK THAT GOD APPROVES OF YOUR BLIND SPOTS

Don't ever think God is going to say, "Oh, I'm sorry, that was one of your blind spots. That sin doesn't count." As certainly as we are held responsible for blatant sin, we are held responsible for blind-spot sin.

David's blind spot led to Scripture's most infamous act of adultery. David took Bathsheba, another man's wife. And one sin led to another in the cover-up process. (We will consider this story in chapter 9.) Sadly, after his sin, confession, and forgiveness, David's life was never the same. Sin carries serious consequences. David's family was plagued by jealousy, conflict, and power struggles. His children experienced the tragedy of rape and murder. At one point, Absalom, his son, conspired against him and ran David out of the kingdom. Finally Absalom was killed in battle and David returned to Jerusalem. But he sat on the throne with a broken heart. David knew his son's death was a result of his sin.

Unfortunately, blind spots live on. If not handled they may well be passed to our children. David's son Solomon succeeded him as king, but the kingdom was not the only thing he inherited from David.

> King Solomon, however, loved many foreign women besides Pharaoh's daughter—Moabites, Ammonites, Edomites, Sidonians and Hittites. They were from nations about which the LORD had told the Israelites, "You must not intermarry with them, because they will surely turn your hearts after their gods." Nevertheless, Solomon held fast to them in love. He had seven hundred wives of royal birth and three hundred concubines, and his wives led him astray. As Solomon grew old, his wives turned his heart after other gods, and his heart was

not fully devoted to the Lord his God, as the heart
of David his father had been.

—1 Kings 11:1–4

Solomon allowed his blind spot to turn his heart from God.
After Solomon, the nation was divided again. Israel's united
kingdom, the thing for which David had waited so long, lasted
only two generations, due in part to David's blind spots.

Killing a Gnat with a Sledgehammer

Sometimes we have blind spots that become character issues. We have considered such a blind spot with David's too-
many wives. But other times we have blind-spot moments. The
emotion of the moment drives us to act out of character, but
the results are devastating nonetheless. Let's consider another
blind spot in David's life, but this time an out-of-character
blind-spot moment.

David and his men were making their way down to the
Desert of Maon. A wealthy man named Nabal lived in the area
with his wife, Abigail. Nabal was "surly and mean" and his wife
was "intelligent and beautiful." David sent his men to Nabel
with these instructions:

> "Say to him: 'Long life to you! Good health to
> you and your household! And good health to all
> that is yours! Now I hear that it is sheep-shearing
> time. When your shepherds were with us, we did
> not mistreat them, and the whole time they were
> at Carmel nothing of theirs was missing. Ask your
> own servants and they will tell you. Therefore be
> favorable toward my young men, since we come at
> a festive time. Please give your servants and your
> son David whatever you can find for them.'" When
> David's men arrived, they gave Nabal this message

in David's name. Then they waited. Nabal answered David's servants, "Who is this David? Who is this son of Jesse? Many servants are breaking away from their masters these days. Why should I take my bread and water, and the meat I have slaughtered for my shearers, and give it to men coming from who knows where?" David's men turned around and went back. When they arrived, they reported every word.

—1 Samuel 25:6–12

When he heard the news, David had a blind-spot moment. He said to his men, "'Put on your swords!' So they put on their swords, and David put on his. About four hundred men went up with David, while two hundred stayed with the supplies" (1 Sam. 25:13).

Four hundred fighting soldiers against a bunch of sheep-shearers? Quite a show of force! Certainly, Nabal was "surly and mean," but did David really need four hundred soldiers? Talk about going after a gnat with a sledgehammer. David, do you think you might be overreacting?

There are times when we have had it "up to here." Our nerves are frayed. The pressure is on. We are tired. We are in no mood for answers we don't want. Like a match put to a fuse, we sizzle and blow like Mount Vesuvius. The blind-spot moment of overreaction can get ugly and leave some debris. In these moments we need someone to settle us down. For David that "someone" was Nabal's wife, Abigail.

One of the servants told Nabal's wife Abigail: "David sent messengers from the desert to give our master his greetings, but he hurled insults at them. Yet these men were very good to us. They did not mistreat us, and the whole time we were out in the fields near them nothing was missing. Night and day they were a wall around us all the time we were herding our sheep near them. Now think it over and see what you can do, because disaster is hanging over our master and his whole household. He is such a wicked man that no one can talk to him." Abigail lost no time. She took two hundred loaves of bread, two skins of wine, five dressed sheep, five seahs of roasted grain, a hundred cakes of raisins and two hundred cakes of pressed figs, and loaded them on donkeys. Then she told her servants, "Go on ahead; I'll follow you." But she did not tell her husband Nabal. As she came riding her donkey into a mountain ravine, there were David and his men descending toward her, and she met them. David had just said, "It's been useless—all my watching over this fellow's property in the desert so that nothing of his was missing. He has paid me back evil for good. May God deal with David, be it ever so severely, if by morning I leave alive one male of all who belong to him!"

—1 Samuel 25:14–22

Thank God for Abigail! She saved David from a regrettable mistake. When she heard what had happened and what was about to happen, she "lost no time." She lit the afterburners and loaded the bread, wine, sheep, grain, raisin cakes, and pressed figs on the donkeys. She set out to stop a disaster. David thanked God for sending Abigail.

David said to Abigail, "Praise be to the LORD, the God of Israel, who has sent you today to meet me. May you be blessed for your good judgment and for keeping me from bloodshed this day and from avenging myself with my own hands. Otherwise, as surely as the LORD, the God of Israel, lives, who has kept me from harming you, if you had not come quickly to meet me, not one male belonging to Nabal would have been left alive by daybreak." Then David accepted from her hand what she had brought him and said, "Go home in peace. I have heard your words and granted your request."

—1 Samuel 25:32–35

WIN ONE, LOSE ONE

After her save, Abigail went back home to find Nabal, oblivious to all that had happened, holding a banquet. He was "very drunk," so Abigail waited until morning to tell him what she had done. When she told him the story "his heart failed him and he became like stone," probably a stroke from the news. Later that day, "the LORD struck Nabal and he died." But now we move back to David's blind spot. When he heard that Nabal was dead he took Abigail as another one of his wives.

David, the man after God's own heart, had a serious blind spot that impacted his character and his children. In addition, he had blind-spot moments like the one we have considered with Nabal. Annoying things, these blind spots. How do we deal with them?

DEALING WITH BLIND SPOTS

Living with blind spots is not acceptable to God. Sooner or later (preferably sooner) we must deal with our blind spots.

Ask God to Point Out the Blind Spots

The psalmist prayed, "Search me, O God, and know [better: make known] my heart; test me and know [make known] my anxious thoughts. See if there is any offensive way in me, and lead me in the way everlasting" (Ps. 139:23–24).

Ignite

Allow God's Word to Point Out the Blind Spots

Psalm 19 explains the benefits of reading the Bible. Scripture, the psalmist notes, makes "wise the simple," gives "joy to the heart," and gives "light to the eyes." In Psalm 19:12, the psalmist asks a rhetorical question: "Who can discern his errors?" In other words, "Who can see his own blind spots?" The answer: no one. That's why it is critical to be in God's Word on a daily basis. The psalmist says it well: "Your word is a lamp to my feet and a light for my path" (Ps. 119:105).

Get Involved in a Church Community

We need to be around people who love us enough to point out our blind spots. The writer to the Hebrews makes it clear that we are to "consider how we may spur one another on toward love and good deeds. Let us not give up meeting together, as some are in the habit of doing, but let us encourage one another—and all the more as you see the Day approaching" (Heb. 10:24–25).

Respond Now!

Has God shined his light on one or more of your blind spots? Deal with those problem areas right now. God loves you too much to let you live with an area of blindness. Take action before God does. His wake-up calls can be pretty severe.

A PERSONAL BLIND-SPOT CONFESSION

I have coached my children's recreational teams in our community. I hate to admit it, but for many years I was a downright jerk. Now, years removed from my coaching "jerkiness," it's hard to believe that I took winning so seriously. But I did. Several of us coaches worked hard at beating each other.

Somehow we forgot about the kids. At least I did. I wish I could have a "do-over" on those years, but I can't.

I was very hard on my own children as well. I put so much pressure on them that they were unable to enjoy the sports they loved. My blind-spot-wake-up-call came one day when I berated my daughter for striking out. Here is the story from my side and then my daughter's side. I wrote with Paul's words from Colossians 3:21 ringing in my head, "Fathers, do not embitter your children, or they will become discouraged."

My Perspective

From the time that I was seven years old, it was drilled into my head. Every coach from ten-and-under to college bellowed the same command: "Don't take a called third strike! If you strike out, you had better go down swinging. When you have two strikes, widen your stance, choke up a bit, protect the plate. Whatever you do, never watch the third strike go by!" So when I began coaching my kids, I repeated the same instruction.

I will never forget one particular softball game. My oldest daughter, Brittany, a fifth grader at the time and a great player, made the last out of the game by taking a called third strike. My insides ignited. After the obligatory handshakes and post-game "great game, girls" talk, I walked to the car with Brittany. The very second the doors were shut, I exploded. "What just happened out there? Why didn't you swing the bat? Never, I mean never, take a called third strike. How many times have you heard me say that? You could have pulled that pitch down the right field line. As fast as you are, you could have made it to third easily. We could have won the game! What were you doing?" I stopped to take a breath and then started repeating the questions with a louder voice. Then I saw the tears. My heart sank and I realized how foolish I had been to get so upset with my daughter over a recreational softball game.

Please don't do what I did. Do not embitter your children. The word *embitter* means to "irritate" or "provoke." One translation used the word "exasperate." This continued practice will cause them to lose heart and confidence and respect in you as a father. As fathers we are called to demonstrate what it means to honor the heavenly Father in all things. As fathers we are called to build up our children. As fathers we are called to demonstrate unconditional acceptance and love. Embittered hearts will walk away from God and us.

Brittany's Perspective

The walk back to the car might have been worse than the actual strikeout. Check that statement. It was infinitely worse. When I think of bad games, none stick out in my mind like that particular one—my at-bats consisted of nothing but strikeouts and in-field pop-flies. Never in my five years of playing had I struck out so much in one game. Usually, I was not one to watch a ball pass by (I was notorious for swinging at the first pitch). During this particular at bat, I was horrified to hear the umpire—an energetic baseball enthusiast whose "strike" call always made us jump—call "staaariike three! She's out!" From my left-handed batting stance, my dad in his third base coach position was directly in my line of sight. My stomach flip-flopped as I, anxiously glancing up the third base line, saw my dad drop his head. Game over.

I walked numbly to our old gray Honda, dragging my cleated feet against the pavement, dreading the car ride home. My mom, who had driven separately, passed by on her way to the van. "See you at home," she said, giving me an empathetic glance and my arm a reassuring squeeze.

"Bye, Mom," I managed to choke out, while in my head I was screaming, "Please! Ask to take me home! I don't want to drive home with Dad!" But, unable to read my thoughts, my mom walked away, and I was left to face the terrible silence preceding whatever my dad had to say in response to my "unacceptable" softball behavior. I don't remember everything he said, but I didn't cry often as a child. I cried on that car ride home. And then I cried more once I got home. But once I got out of the bathroom (I took a "shower" so that I could sit in the bathroom and cry some more), my dad was right there, waiting to apologize and to console me.

Those were some intense softball years. We can look back on those years and laugh at the ridiculous level of intensity, but up through the seventh grade, recreational softball was competitive—to put it lightly. Winning was king, and I remember feeling discouraged on many counts when I felt like I had let my dad down. Softball was more nerve-racking than fun. I was always nervous that I would mess up and disappoint my dad. Don't get me wrong. My dad was a great coach. He was great at teaching the fundamentals, knew fun drills, and was enjoyable to be around. But when the subject of bitterness comes up, those softball years always resurface. I'm really not bitter about it now, but Colossians 3:21 brings up a good point. I think that becoming "embittered," or to be made to feel troubled or distressed, is something that a lot of children struggle with.

No matter your age, when one feels like he has not lived up to his parents' expectations—not gotten the grades, made the cut, landed the job—it can be really discouraging. And while I think having high expectations for your children is completely justifiable, (after all, they're your kids, you should want the very best for them!), loving us (not necessarily "tough love!") through our failures is vital for our emotional well-being.

I have never—not even for a tenth of a second—doubted that my dad loves me, but that didn't stop me from feeling anxious before softball games. I can't tell you how many times my dad has asked me to forgive him for his years of ultra-competitive softball coaching. And I'm totally over it (it's great to have something to hold over his head, though!). But since realizing his mixed-up priorities, my dad has been nothing but encouraging in my various sports endeavors. He wasn't my coach while I played in high school, but I always enjoyed having him at my games. If I'm discouraged, he's always there to support me.

In the seventh grade, the last year he coached my team, we won the championship. Winning the championship should have been exciting, but once again, I was in tears on the way home. This time I was disappointed in my own performance. But to this day, my dad still reminds me of the vital role I played in those games. Without my parents' support through my years of softball, various sports, and other activities, I don't know where I'd be. It might sound strange, but I really think that going through those years of intensity, and then realizing that we had our eyes on the wrong prize, created a stronger bond between us. We were both able to grow as a result of seeing how our priorities were out of whack, and I think we're closer because of it.

This past summer, I had the chance to help my dad coach my younger sister's third and fourth grade softball team. Getting to coach alongside Dad was a blast, and it's so fun to see how laid back he's become (youngest child syndrome). On multiple occasions, after playing against a team with an intense coach, we would laugh most of the way home, the conversation usually starting off with, "Who did that coach in the purple shirt remind you of?"

I wish I could say that was the last time I blew it with my children. I have had to go to each one of them more than once to ask for forgiveness as well as asking forgiveness from my Father. That event happened over a decade ago, and by God's grace, Brittany and I have a great relationship. She even has a touch of my sarcastic humor. And sometimes right out of the blue she'll say, "Hey, Dad, do you remember that time you made me cry in the car after that softball game?" Then she lets out her patented chuckle.

Hand your blind spots to God. He will open your eyes and ignite your heart with a burning passion to follow hard after him.

Father, don't let me live with blind spots. Please point them out to me now. Bring others into my life who are bold enough to bring them to my attention.
Don't let my blind spot cause me to crash. Reveal it. Remove it. Restore me to clarity and focus.
I pray for your intervention in Christ's name.
Amen.

Chapter 8

Igniting an Obedient Heart

> It does not matter how small the sins are, provided
> that their cumulative effect is to edge the man away
> from the Light and out into the Nothing. Murder is
> no better than cards if cards can do the trick. Indeed,
> the safest road to Hell is the gradual one—the gentle
> slope, soft underfoot, without sudden turnings, without
> milestones, without signposts.
>
> —C. S. Lewis
> *The Screwtape Letters*

David is king over the entire nation of Israel. He is experiencing God's blessing and success. In a very strategic
battle, David and his men captured the city of Jerusalem. It
is now called the "City of David." The Philistines, the sworn
enemy of God's people, have been defeated. There is peace and
security in the land. Everything is complete . . . well, almost
everything.

There is actually one last piece of the puzzle that needs to
be put in place to finish the whole picture of this nation under
God.

> David again brought together out of Israel chosen
> men, thirty thousand in all. He and all his men set
> out from Baalah of Judah to bring up from there
> the ark of God, which is called by the Name, the
> name of the LORD Almighty, who is enthroned
> between the cherubim that are on the ark.
>
> —2 Samuel 6:1–2

In the New Testament, the Spirit of God dwells in the heart of every believer. Paul tells believers that we are the "temple of the Holy Spirit" (1 Cor. 6:19). But things were different before the Holy Spirit came in Acts 2. In the Old Testament there were many signs and symbols that pointed to God and represented him. The temple was the place where worshippers went to meet with God and in the temple was the ark of the covenant.

Three hundred years before David, God instructed Moses to build the ark and gave him some very specific instructions. The special chest was to be three-and-three-quarter feet long (no longer, no shorter) and two-and-a-quarter feet wide and high (no longer, no shorter). It was to be gold-plated inside and out.

The ark was God's treasure chest. It served as a physical, visible reminder of his work among the people. The ark was designed to remind the people of five things . . .

God's Instruction. The stone tablets of the Law, the Ten Commandments, were placed inside the ark.

God's Provision. A two-quart pot of manna was placed inside the chest. The manna was a reminder that God had provided food for his people during their years of wandering in the desert.

God's Protection. The rod that belonged to Aaron, the first priest, was placed inside the ark. God used the rod of Aaron in judging the sons of Korah who rebelled against Moses. The rod was a reminder of God's protection and a warning against rebellion.

God's Presence. On the top of the gold-plated lid there were two cherubim or angel-like figures. The two figures sat on either end of the lid and faced each other. At certain times God would appear in the form of a cloud or mist and remain between the cherubim. These figures were a reminder of his presence among the people.

God's Forgiveness, Grace, and Mercy. Each year the high priest would go before the ark and offer sacrifices for himself and the people. He would sprinkle the blood of a sacrificed animal on the lid, which was also known as the "mercy seat." On this special Day of Atonement (Yom Kippur) the people would be forgiven of their sins.

The ark was the tangible object of Israel's worship. It served as a visible reminder of the invisible God. The ark represented the person and character of God. Special instruction had been given regarding its care and handling. There was only one problem: The ark had not been central in Israel's worship for the past forty years. Saul was busy chasing David and had allowed the spiritual climate of the country to slide. But now David was in charge. One of the first things he did was to get the ark and bring it to Jerusalem. David desired that this visible representation of the person and work of God be given a place of prominence in the nation.

> They set the ark of God on a new cart and brought
> it from the house of Abinadab, which was on the

hill. Uzzah and Ahio, sons of Abinadab, were
guiding the new cart with the ark of God on it,
and Ahio was walking in front of it. David and the
whole house of Israel were celebrating with all their
might before the LORD, with songs and with harps,
lyres, tambourines, sistrums and cymbals.

—2 Samuel 6:3–5

Take a minute to picture the scene in your mind. The ark
is on a new cart. It is being pulled by oxen. David and the
whole house of Israel—thousands of people—were celebrating
with all their might. The people are going crazy . . . for the
Lord. Finally the ark will be returned to its rightful place. The
sound of shouting and singing and the playing of harps, lyres,
tambourines, and cymbals was deafening. But wait a second!

When they came to the threshing floor of Nacon,
Uzzah reached out and took hold of the ark of
God, because the oxen stumbled. The LORD's anger
burned against Uzzah because of his irreverent act;
therefore God struck him down and he died there
beside the ark of God.

—2 Samuel 6:6–7

Suddenly the shouting turns to silence. Right in the middle
of great celebration, a worshipper lays dead by the ark, "struck
down" by God. One minute Uzzah is singing; the next minute
he is still. The whole incident begs a question: Why in the world
would God do that? Uzzah thought the ark was going to fall,
for goodness sake! He was trying to help. God, to be honest, it
kind of makes me want to stay at a distance.

Then David was angry because the LORD's wrath
had broken out against Uzzah, and to this day that
place is called Perez Uzzah. David was afraid of the

LORD that day and said, "How can the ark of the
LORD ever come to me?" He was not willing to take
the ark of the LORD to be with him in the City
of David. Instead, he took it aside to the house of
Obed-Edom the Gittite.

—2 Samuel 6:8–10

Before we consider what happened next, let's take some
time to follow the extremes of emotion this incident presents.
David's emotions moved from great excitement and anticipation to anger. He couldn't wait to get the ark to Jerusalem;
now he refuses to take it into the city. David moves from "I
have to have God with me" to "I don't know if I want you with
me." Uncontainable happiness turns to unbelievable horror.
The celebration ends early. The musical instruments are packed
up. David and the people of Israel leave the cart at the house of
Obed-Edom and walk back to Jerusalem with their heads down
and their hearts confused. The whole thing is a little confusing,
isn't it? Until we include a very important detail.

In Exodus 25 and Numbers 4, God gave specific teaching
regarding the transport of the ark. Note the instruction:

Cast four gold rings for it and fasten them to its
four feet, with two rings on one side and two rings
on the other. Then make poles of acacia wood and
overlay them with gold. Insert the poles into the
rings on the sides of the chest to carry it. The poles
are to remain in the rings of this ark; they are not
to be removed.

—Exodus 25:12–15

Furthermore, Numbers 4 explains that only the Kohathites
were to carry the ark. Kohath was the second son of Levi and
his ancestors were given this special assignment with specific
instructions.

> After Aaron and his sons have finished covering the
> holy furnishings and all the holy articles, and when
> the camp is ready to move, the Kohathites are to
> come to do the carrying. But they must not touch
> the holy things or they will die. The Kohathites
> are to carry those things that are in the Tent of
> Meeting.
>
> —Numbers 4:15

Did you note the punishment for touching the ark? Death.
Now the whole thing with Uzzah is starting to make sense.
Remember, David and his men "set the ark of God on a new
cart and brought it from the house of Abinadab, which was on
the hill. Uzzah and Ahio, sons of Abinadab, were guiding the
new cart" (2 Sam. 6:3).

The ark was to be carried by poles, not on a cart, even a new
cart. The ark was to be carried by the descendants of Kohath,
not the sons of Abinadab. David was following the way the
Philistines moved the ark from city to city. He was using the
most expedient way—the Philistine way—instead of God's
way.

OBEDIENCE . . . EVEN IN THE DETAILS

God takes his instruction seriously. He does not waste his
inspired breath. He expects things to be done his way, the right
way.

Failure to do what God asks may be caused by many things.
Some disobedience comes as a result of ignorance. We are not
aware of a certain instruction. Sometimes we choose not to take
God's Word seriously. Remember what Satan said to Eve when
she explained that death would result from touching the fruit of
the tree in the middle of the garden? "You will surely not die,"
the serpent said to the woman. And sometimes we are simply

unwilling to subject ourselves to God's instruction. Whatever our reasons or excuses, God's standard is "The Standard." He demands obedience even in the small things.

C. S. Lewis's book *The Screwtape Letters* is about a senior devil instructing a junior devil on the art of temptation. The senior devil has some profound instructions regarding "small" sins.

> It does not matter how small the sins are, provided that their cumulative effect is to edge the man away from the Light and out into the Nothing. Murder is no better than cards if cards can do the trick. Indeed, the safest road to Hell is the gradual one—the gentle slope, soft underfoot, without sudden turnings, without milestones, without signposts.[1]

For David, and us, small sins become big misses. I don't know why David moved the ark the wrong way. Maybe he didn't know any better. But that's not an excuse. He was the leader of God's people moving the tangible reminder of God's presence. Maybe it was a matter of expediency. He wanted to get the ark to Jerusalem, and a cart pulled by oxen was certainly faster than men carrying it up and down the countryside.

I don't know why David missed the details of obedience, but then, I don't know why a man begins an "innocent" relationship. A lingering look. A touch. A little too personal conversation. Some flirting texts. Small stuff? Not at all. It's the "gentle slope" to adultery and blowing up his family.

I don't know why David missed the details of moving the ark, but then, I don't know why people will risk their reputation by telling just a little "white lie." We need to remember that God doesn't color code our deceptions.

I don't know why David missed the details, but then, I don't know why a person will risk his job by padding the books "just a little." The heavy consequences can't be worth adding a little bit here and cutting a little bit there.

I don't know why David disobeyed, but then I don't understand why a person sings praises to God each Sunday and chases after the almighty dollar all week. Since when did bigger and better equal spirituality? "Providing for my family" and greed are too often synonymous terms.

I don't know why David missed the small things, but then I don't understand how Christians let patriotism sneak into their doctrine and allow it to become an essential. Quoting again from *The Screwtape Letters*, the senior devil, Screwtape, has this advice regarding the believer and patriotism for his nephew and junior devil in training.

> Let [the Christian] begin treating Patriotism . . . as a part of his religion. Then let him, under the influence of partisan spirit, come to regard it as the most important part. Then quietly and gradually nurse him on to the stage at which the religion becomes merely part of the "Cause," in which Christianity is valued chiefly because of the excellent arguments it can produce. . . . Once you have made the World an end, and faith a means, you have almost won your man, and it makes very little difference what kind of worldly end he is pursuing. Provided that meetings, pamphlets, policies, movements, causes, and crusades, matter more to him than prayers and sacraments and charity, he is ours—and the more "religious" (on those terms), the more securely ours. I can show you a pretty cageful down here.
>
> Your affectionate uncle
> SCREWTAPE[2]

How can we be so close to the flame, but live so far from the heat? It's the small misses. The small sins. Carrying the right thing the wrong way. Someone has said that excellence is in the details. God says throughout his Word that obedience is in the details. Perhaps it's time for us to go through a great relearning. Relearning that God is holy. Relearning that his Word is perfect. Relearning that all his instruction must be taken seriously. Relearning that the cumulative effect of "little" sins is every bit as devastating as "big" sins.

How Are You Doing in the Little Things?

Take the time to do a pie chart of your life. Label the major sections—God, Marriage, Children, Work, Service, etc. Then break down each area.

God

- Word—Scripture reading and prayer
- Worship—personal and corporate
- Connect—meaningful fellowship with other believers
- Serve—use of gifts
- Share—telling others about Jesus

Marriage

- Reading Scripture and praying together
- Worshipping together
- Enrichment activities such as seminars or conferences
- Making a covenant with our eyes not to look lustfully at a woman (or longingly at a man)

You get the idea. Break down each area. Then take some time to prayerfully see how you are doing . . . in the details . . . in the small things. As God reveals areas you need to change, do something. Change! One more quote from *The Screwtape Letters*:

The great thing is to prevent his doing anything. As long as he does not convert it into action, it does not matter how much he thinks about this new repentance. Let the little brute wallow in it. Let him, if he has any bent that way, write a book about it; that is often an excellent way of sterilizing the seeds which the Enemy [God] plants in a human soul. Let him do anything but act. No amount of piety in his imagination and affections will harm us if we can keep it out of his will. As one of the humans has said, active habits are strengthened by repetition but passive ones are weakened. The more often he feels without acting, the less he will be able ever to act and, in the long run, the less he will be able to feel.

Your affectionate uncle
SCREWTAPE[3]

MISSING THE BLESSING

David's disobedience caused him to misunderstand God. He was angry that God had put Uzzah to death. He was scared that another "small sin" might result in a big consequence. By this point he understood that he had not followed the instruction on carrying the ark. And he didn't want to miss another detail. So he was content to leave the ark outside of Jerusalem . . . until he realized that he was missing the blessing.

> The ark of the LORD remained in the house of Obed-Edom the Gittite for three months, and the LORD blessed him and his entire household. Now King David was told, "The LORD has blessed the household of Obed-Edom and everything he has, because of the ark of God."
> —2 Samuel 6:11–12a

We don't know who told David the news, but their message is clear: "Hey, David, have you heard? The entire household of Obed-Edom is receiving some serious blessings from God! Maybe, David, and of course you are the king so this is entirely up to you, but maybe, we should take another shot at bringing the ark to Jerusalem." David agreed. But this time David made sure he did it God's way. And God honored his desires. He ignited David's heart with a burning passion for obedience . . . even in the details.

> So David went down and brought up the ark of God from the house of Obed-Edom to the City of David with rejoicing. When those who were carrying the ark of the LORD had taken six steps, he sacrificed a bull and a fattened calf. David, wearing a linen ephod, danced before the LORD with all his might, while he and the entire house of Israel brought up the ark of the LORD with shouts and the sound of trumpets.
>
> —2 Samuel 6:12b–15

SECOND CHANCES

Maybe you have missed a few details of obedience. To be sure, there are always consequences to sin, even "small" sin. But here's some good news: God is a God of second chances. You may have done it your way the first time around and have the scars to prove it. Now you can do it God's way. Confess your sin and failure and anger and confusion to God. Ask him for the desire to change. Tell him that you don't want to miss his blessings. Commit to live in obedience. Get ready. He will ignite your heart with a burning passion for obedience and you can dance before the Lord with all your might!

Father, keep our hearts tender to small sins. Help us to never do what is expedient. May we always be committed to do what is right even when it hurts, even when it slows down our plans, even when it is costly. Give us a burning passion to obey you . . . even in the details.
For Christ's sake.
Amen.

Chapter 9

Igniting a Fallen Heart

I never, ever anticipated being unfaithful to my wife . . . NEVER . . . and I was in total shock, as well as disbelief, when it happened. My own parents are divorced, and so I have always had an inner motivation and determination to have a successful marriage, and to become a model husband and father. If you would have predicted that I was going to have an extramarital affair, I would have told you that you were crazy. I have always considered myself to be one of the least likely people ever to fall prey to this terrible sin.

These words were written by a friend of mine after his fall into immorality. By God's grace the affair ended, his relationship with his wife was restored, and now he is able to help others who have taken the same path. Not everyone is so blessed. Many families have been blown to pieces by a father or a mother heading down the path the writer of the Proverbs likens to "an ox going to the slaughter," "a deer stepping in a noose," or "a bird darting into a snare" (Prov. 7:22–23). As my friend notes, this happens to some of the "least likely people." It even happened to a man after God's own heart.

WRONG PLACE, WRONG TIME

After years of running from Saul and waiting for the promised crown, David is now fully established as Israel's king. He is around fifty years old and has been the king of Israel for twenty years. In these two decades David proved himself as a strong and successful ruler. The divided people of Judah and Israel have now been brought together into one united kingdom. David has wise advisors around him. He has built a strong army. He has never been defeated on the battlefield. The country is economically strong.

Israel is strong spiritually as well. David, the man after God's own heart, continues to write songs. Some are didactic to teach the people who God is. Others are songs of praise purposed to lead the people in worship. Plans are being made to build a beautiful temple to honor the Lord.

In Israel's last military campaign, David and his men drove the aggressive Ammonites back to their capital city of Rabbah. Then winter set in and the military campaign ground to a halt during the months of inclement weather. But now the winter is over.

In the Middle East the month of March marks the end of the rainy season. It is during this time of the year that the roads become passable again. The spring will provide plenty of food for the warhorses and pack animals. Foot soldiers will be able to raid the fields for food. So, David sent Joab, the army commander, and his men to finish the job they had started with the Ammonites.

> In the spring, at the time when kings go off to war, David sent Joab out with the king's men and the whole Israelite army. They destroyed the Ammonites and besieged Rabbah. But David remained in Jerusalem.
>
> —2 Samuel 11:1

We are not told why David chose to stay in Jerusalem. We do know that this was not David's normal practice. The major responsibility for a king is to lead his men into war. And David is normally there leading the charge (see 2 Sam. 5:6–25; 8:1–14; 10:1–19). But this particular spring, he stayed home.

Remember it's spring and the weather is nice and warm. In this day of no air conditioning, bedrooms were built on the top floor of a home so that the cool evening breeze would flow through the open windows of the room. Often patios were built off of the bedrooms. The height of the patios would provide privacy. In David's palace, the patio would have been decorated with fine furnishings and served as a meeting place for advisors.

For whatever reason, one night David could not sleep. So he "got up from his bed and walked around on the roof of the palace. From the roof he saw a woman bathing. The woman was very beautiful, and David sent someone to find out about her" (2 Sam. 11:2–3a).

It was not unusual for people to bathe outside in the confines of their private courtyard. Private, of course, unless someone from the roof of the palace is looking down on you.

The words "very beautiful," used to describe the woman, are reserved to describe a striking physical appearance. She was more than attractive. She was gorgeous in face and form. And David was intrigued and sent a person to find out about her. The messenger forms his response in a question, attempting to help David see the dangerous inquiry. "Isn't this Bathsheba, the daughter of Eliam and the wife of Uriah the Hittite?" (2 Sam. 11:3). The messenger had no question as to what was on David's mind. Can you hear him slow down his speech and raise his tone when he says, "the wife of Uriah the Hittite?" In effect, the messenger says, "David, don't do what you are thinking about doing!" It is also important to note that the father and husband of Bathsheba are members of David's elite soldiers, his "Mighty Men" (2 Sam. 23:34, 39). They were the best of the best, the crème de la crème. They were loyal to the king and lived to fight for him. In fact, they were out fighting for him on that warm spring evening. There are two more important connections that should have given David reason to pause. Bathsheba's father, Eliam, was the son of Ahithophel, David's counselor (1 Chron. 27:33). Bathsheba is the granddaughter of one of David's chief advisors! But, as in all acts of lust, David throws reason out the window.

Tim Stafford, writing in *Christianity Today*, explains the dangerous process David is engaged in.

> The psychology of lust is a simple process: it begins with attraction; it turns quickly to dissatisfaction; it results in fixation. It leaves us ungrateful, discontented, and obsessive. When you are filled with lust . . . you can have nothing in your mind but that appetite for what you lack.

Stafford adds,

> This is not just true of sex. Power. Pleasure. Wealth. Possession. And attraction to what you see. A dissatisfaction with what you have. A fixation on getting what you want.[1]

David was fixated on Bathsheba. And no doubt she was flattered by his invitation. In a moment of premeditated passion—at least on David's part—they slept together. The sin took on a life of its own—literally. Bathsheba "conceived and sent word to David, saying, 'I am pregnant'" (2 Sam. 11:5).

At the end of 2 Samuel 11:4, the writer adds an instructive parenthetical comment: "[Bathsheba] had purified herself from her uncleanness." This short sentence provides two important points. First, Bathsheba's time of the month was completed, so she wasn't pregnant prior to her encounter with David. It was definitely the king's child. Second, since her time of the month was complete, she was at a time of high percentage regarding pregnancy. Caution and reason were jettisoned (they always are) in the midst of unbridled lust.

Would this sin have been just as wrong if Bathsheba had not become pregnant? Yes! But now the secret is going public. And David put a cover-up plan into action.

> So David sent this word to Joab: "Send me Uriah the Hittite." And Joab sent him to David. When Uriah came to him, David asked him how Joab was, how the soldiers were and how the war was going.
> —2 Samuel 11:6–7

Can't you just picture the scene? Uriah, straight from the field, is ushered into the palace for some food and refreshments. As he sits down to enjoy some fresh fruit, David, whose mind has been turned from his army at war, pretends to care about what is happening in the battle. His pretense is built around a series of questions: "How is Joab? Is he encouraged? Is he healthy? How is the morale of the soldiers? How is the food holding out? Do you need anything? How is the war going? Are we meeting our objectives? Any unexpected turns?" All pretense! Sin and its cover-up make us a fake. David is not concerned about Joab, the soldiers, or the war. The conversation drips with hypocrisy. But that's what happens when one is living in secret sin.

So the cover-up plan begins. David thanks Uriah for coming and instructs him to go home and relax. The unspoken implication is clear—Uriah, enjoy your beautiful wife. When Uriah left the palace, "a gift from the king was sent after him" (2 Sam. 11:8). I wonder what the gift was. I cannot help but think it was something to encourage a passionate union. But Uriah did not go home. He slept at the door of the palace.

> When David was told, "Uriah did not go home," he
> asked him, "Haven't you just come from a distance?
> Why didn't you go home?" Uriah said to David,
> "The ark and Israel and Judah are staying in tents,
> and my master Joab and my lord's men are camped
> in the open fields. How could I go to my house to
> eat and drink and lie with my wife? As surely as you
> live, I will not do such a thing!"
>
> —2 Samuel 11:10–11

Can you imagine how those words must have stung? Without
knowing it, Uriah was emphasizing David's despicable act of
having an intimate encounter with a soldier's wife while the
soldier was on the battlefield. His reference to Bathsheba as
"my wife," again unknowingly, emphasizes that David broke
the seventh and tenth commandments!

When you come face-to-face with your sin there are only
two options: confession or cover-up. David, not willing to
confess, moves to the second phase of his cover-up plan.

> Then David said to him, "Stay here one more day,
> and tomorrow I will send you back." So Uriah
> remained in Jerusalem that day and the next. At
> David's invitation, he ate and drank with him, and
> David made him drunk. But in the evening Uriah
> went out to sleep on his mat among his master's
> servants; he did not go home.
>
> —2 Samuel 11:12–13

David moved into phase three. He wrote a note to Joab instructing the commander to put Uriah on the front line where
the fighting was the fiercest. Then Joab was to instruct a sudden
withdrawal without Uriah getting the word. David stamped
his official seal on the plan and gave it to Uriah. The honorable
soldier took his death warrant and handed it to Joab.

David and Joab had a tense relationship. Men of power often do. Joab didn't like David's plan. No doubt, some questions would be asked if Uriah was left alone to die. So he sent some men close to the wall of Rabbah they had under siege. At this dangerous position the men were in the range of arrows and catapulted stones. Many soldiers lost their lives that day, including Uriah the Hittite, husband of Bathsheba. For David, the problem was solved, or so he thought.

Believers are not immune to sin. While the ultimate penalty of sin is gone through Christ, the propensity to sin remains. The doctrine of Original Sin says that at birth each one of us has the seeds of sin in our heart just waiting for a time and opportunity to sprout and grow. To put it another way, we are not sinners because we sin; we sin because we are sinners. Each of us must address our fallen heart.

In his book *Temptation*, Dietrich Bonhoeffer addresses the issue:

> In our members there is a slumbering inclination toward desire, which is both sudden and fierce. With irresistible power, desire seizes mastery of the flesh. All at once a secret, smoldering fire is kindled. The flesh burns and is in flames. It makes no difference whether it is a sexual desire, or ambition, or vanity, or desire for revenge, or love of fame and power, or greed for money. . . .
>
> At this moment God is quite unreal to us, he loses all reality, and only desire for the creature is real; the only reality is the devil. Satan does not fill us with hatred of God, but with forgetfulness of God.[2]

Burning with lust, David followed the all-too-familiar pattern of sin that started with Adam and Eve in the garden: He saw; he wanted; he took. For the moment, David forgot God.

117

Ignite

The fallen heart cannot be self-ignited. God sends help. Our task is to listen to the message and the messenger.

DON'T REJECT THE MESSENGER

David married Uriah's widow. A month went by, then two months, then nine months. Bathsheba gave birth to a baby boy. During this time, David never dealt with his sin. Then one day God said, "Time for a wake-up call." The Lord sent a man named Nathan to David. And Nathan grabbed David's attention with a story.

> "There were two men in a certain town, one rich and the other poor. The rich man had a very large number of sheep and cattle, but the poor man had nothing except one little ewe lamb he had bought. He raised it, and it grew up with him and his children. It shared his food, drank from his cup and even slept in his arms. It was like a daughter to him. Now a traveler came to the rich man, but the rich man refrained from taking one of his own sheep or cattle to prepare a meal for the traveler who had come to him. Instead, he took the ewe lamb that belonged to the poor man and prepared it for the one who had come to him." David burned with anger against the man and said to Nathan, "As surely as the LORD lives, the man who did this deserves to die! He must pay for that lamb four times over, because he did such a thing and had no pity." Then Nathan said to David, "You are the man!"
> —2 Samuel 12:1–7

The fallen heart can become hard and calloused. For at least nine months David lived with his unrepentant sins of coveting another man's wife, stealing, adultery, lying, and murder.

118

It took God's Spirit working through a courageous prophet with a prayerfully constructed emotional story to prick David's heart. The gravity of his sin finally set in when David heard, "You are the man!"

GODLY SORROW OR WORLDLY SORROW

In his second letter to the Corinthians, Paul explains that there are two kinds of sorrow. "Worldly sorrow" is a selfish "I'm sorry I got caught" sorrow. It involves the embarrassment of a private sin becoming public, the regret of hurting loved ones, frustration about having to make a choice to continue or stop the sinful situation, and anger regarding the consequences. Paul is clear that "worldly sorrow brings death" (2 Cor. 7:10b). In this life we will sin. But if our response is self-centered sorrow, and we continue in the sin, our relationship with the Lord has to be held in question. According to John, "No one who is born of God will continue to sin, because God's seed remains in him; he cannot go on sinning, because he has been born of God" (1 John 3:9).

On the other hand, "Godly sorrow brings repentance that leads to salvation and leaves no regret. . . ." Godly sorrow is God-centered. It produces an eagerness to clear ourselves, an indignation and alarm regarding our sin, and a "readiness to see justice done" (2 Cor. 7:10–11).

Don't miss the contrast: Worldly, self-centered sorrow leaves us wallowing in sin and self-pity and reveals a hardened heart that does not know God. Godly sorrow leaves us broken because we have sinned against God and leads to repentance— leaving the path of sin and returning to follow hard after God. Godly sorrow is true repentance.

David's godly sorrow is powerfully revealed in his prayer of repentance recorded in Psalm 51. Let's work our way through this prayer and discover important lessons of true repentance. If you have sinned and desire that God ignite your fallen heart, make this prayer your own.

PSALM 51

For the director of music. A psalm of David. When the prophet Nathan came to him after David had committed adultery with Bathsheba.

1. True repentance is a plea for mercy based on God's unchanging character.

> Have mercy on me, O God, according to your unfailing love; according to your great compassion.
> —Psalm 51:1a

Grace is receiving what we don't deserve. Mercy is not receiving what we do deserve. In the Old Testament the penalty for proven adultery was death. David prays that God spares his life. Repentance begins with a plea for God's mercy. A believer knows that forgiveness is only available by God's grace.

David's prayer is based on two characteristics of God. The Hebrew word *chesed* ("unfailing love") describes the love of covenant that God has with his people. We are told that nothing can separate us from God's love (Rom. 8:38–39). The word *racham* ("compassion") originally carried the idea of the intimate feelings that a mother has for her children. Sinners stand helpless before God. Repentance is a time when we cling to God's unconditional love and his intimate "motherly" compassion he has for his children.

2. True repentance is a plea for complete forgiveness.

> . . . blot out my transgressions. Wash away all my iniquity and cleanse me from my sin.
> —Psalm 51:1b

David asked that his sins be erased like one would blot out the name of a person listed on a register. He desires that his sins are washed away and his heart cleansed. For those of you old enough to have experienced real chalkboards, remember how messy those things used to get? Then one day, usually Mondays, you'd come into the classroom and the board would be spotless. The janitor had sprayed on a cleaner and wiped the board fresh. That's what David is asking God to do. David pleads for complete forgiveness.

3. True repentance acknowledges that all sin is ultimately against God.

> For I know my transgressions, and my sin is always before me. Against you, you only, have I sinned and done what is evil in your sight.
> —Psalm 51:3–4a

David had put off repentance for at least nine months. But he could not forget his sin. For the believer, the convicting work of the Holy Spirit keeps our sin before us. The Spirit reminds us that while our sin hurts others, it is ultimately against God. When David prays, "Against you, you only, have I sinned," he is not forgetting about Bathsheba and Uriah and the others he deceived in his cover-up. He is simply starting at the top with the one who all sin is ultimately against.

4. True repentance accepts the consequences of sin.

> . . . so that you are proved right when you speak
> and justified when you judge.
>   —Psalm 51:4b

Since our sin is ultimately against God, David is ready to accept the consequences. He declares that whatever the consequences, God is right and justified in bringing them. The acceptance of consequences is critical to true repentance. Many have no problem with the pleading for mercy part. They are more than ready for God to bring on the forgiveness. But sin, even forgiven sin, carries consequences. Paul says, "Do not be deceived: God cannot be mocked. A man reaps what he sows" (Gal. 6:7).

After Nathan confronted David in 2 Samuel 12 with the penetrating statement, "You are the man!" he detailed the consequences that God was going to bring. Because David struck down Uriah and stole his wife, God said, "the sword will never depart from your house" (2 Sam. 12:10). In David's lifetime, three of his sons—Amnon, Absalom, and Adonijah—would die violent deaths. But that wasn't all. David's sin had been in secret, but his son's immorality would be in broad daylight "before all Israel" (2 Sam. 12:12).

In response to these severe consequences David confessed, "I have sinned against the LORD." But there was one more consequence that David would have to deal with.

> Nathan replied, "The LORD has taken away your sin. You are not going to die. But because by doing this you have made the enemies of the LORD show utter contempt, the son born to you will die."
>   —2 Samuel 12:13–14

After Nathan left, the son born to David and Bathsheba became ill. David began a period of fasting, spending the nights lying on the ground pleading with God to spare the child. His advisors tried to console him, but he refused their food and stayed prostrate before God.

On the seventh day the child died. David's advisors were scared to tell him the news. They were afraid that David might harm himself. But when he learned of the child's death he got up, washed, changed his clothes, went to the house of the Lord and worshipped, and returned home to eat.

> His servants asked him, "Why are you acting this way? While the child was alive, you fasted and wept, but now that the child is dead, you get up and eat!" He answered, "While the child was still alive, I fasted and wept. I thought, 'Who knows? The LORD may be gracious to me and let the child live.' But now that he is dead, why should I fast? Can I bring him back again? I will go to him, but he will not return to me."
>
> —2 Samuel 12:21–23

This is not the action of a calloused heart or a person in shock after the death of his child. Certainly David experienced the grief of every father who loses a child, compounded by his knowledge that the death was a consequence of sin. This is a man accepting the hard outcome of his sin. He is declaring that God is right when he acts, and just when he judges.

5. True repentance desires a resolve to obey.

> Surely I was sinful at birth, sinful from the time my mother conceived me. Surely you desire truth in the inner parts; you teach me wisdom in the

inmost place. Cleanse me with hyssop, and I will be clean; wash me, and I will be whiter than snow. Let me hear joy and gladness; let the bones you have crushed rejoice. Hide your face from my sins and blot out all my iniquity. Create in me a pure heart, O God, and renew a steadfast spirit within me. Do not cast me from your presence or take your Holy Spirit from me. Restore to me the joy of your salvation and grant me a willing spirit, to sustain me.

—Psalm 51:5–12

David understood the state of the heart. We are born as sinners and our inclination toward sin, even as believers, will dog us until we die. David knows this will not be his last temptation or his last sin. So he prays, not only for his heart to be cleansed, but for a "steadfast" and "willing" spirit to "sustain" his obedience. Sexual sin is a joy sucker! David desires that the joy of his salvation is restored and his resolve is reestablished.

6. A person who is truly repentant desires to help others avoid a fall or be restored from a fall.

Then I will teach transgressors your ways, and sinners will turn back to you. Save me from bloodguilt, O God, the God who saves me, and my tongue will sing of your righteousness. O Lord, open my lips, and my mouth will declare your praise.

—Psalm 51:13–15

David desired to help others turn back from the devastating path that he had taken. He desired to be a humble teacher of God's grace and forgiveness. When we desire to invest in the lives of others so that they can escape the pain we've experienced and caused by our sin, we are truly repentant.

I began this chapter with a quote from a friend who fell into sexual immorality and by God's grace was forgiven and restored. I was preparing to record a radio program about sexual sin, and I asked him to give me some firsthand material. He had told me many times, "If I can ever be of help to others going through the same thing or if I can warn others who are contemplating sexual sin, don't hesitate to call me." He introduced his remarks with these words:

> All men need to realize that they are vulnerable, and that it can happen to them. It can happen to anybody. As a result of my own transgression, I am extremely sensitized to the vulnerability of decent men, and to the temptations we all face. If nothing else, I hope my remarks alert men to the possibility that what happened to me can happen to them. Obviously, I further hope that men listening would take the measure necessary to prevent and avoid the terrible pain that I've experienced and that I've inflicted on others.

Now that is a heart like David's that desires to help others avoid the pitfall of sexual sin.

7. True repentance understands that God is looking for more than lip service.

> You do not delight in sacrifice, or I would bring it; you do not take pleasure in burnt offerings. The sacrifices of God are a broken spirit; a broken and contrite heart, O God, you will not despise.
> —Psalm 51:16–17

David knows that when it comes to repentance, God is looking for more than the sacrifice of a few bulls or an outward show of sorrow. God zeros in on the heart. He is looking for the brokenness that comes when a person understands the gravity of his transgression. God is looking for a remorseful heart that truly regrets even the momentary pleasures of their sin.

8. When true repentance is present, God's presence can bring restoration.

> In your good pleasure make Zion prosper; build up the walls of Jerusalem. Then there will be righteous sacrifices, whole burnt offerings to delight you; then bulls will be offered on your altar.
> —Psalm 51:18–19

David is very aware that his actions have wreaked havoc on his family. He knows that the spiritual state of the king impacted the entire country. So he prayed for a restoration of the walls he had torn down by his sin. He asks God to restore the country to a spiritual awareness of worship and honor to God.

GOD CAN FORGIVE YOUR SIN

There is no sin, or series of sin, that is too great for God to forgive. David, the man after God's own heart, the adulterer, liar, stealer, murderer, coveter, stands forever as a trophy of God's grace and mercy. You can be God's trophy of grace as well. For those who have fallen, I pray that God will ignite your heart with a godly sorrow that leads to repentance. I pray that you will experience his forgiveness and restoration. I pray that he will give you a burning passion to humbly declare his praise.

Dear heavenly Father, grab the hearts of the fallen. Bring conviction on their spirits. Help them to see clearly the error of their ways. By your love that is unfailing and your compassion that is great, listen to the prayers of true repentance. Thank you for the promise to restore and forgive and rebuild the walls that are now broken down.
In Christ's name.
Amen.

Chapter 10

Igniting a Disappointed Heart

The world dwarfs us all, but God dwarfs the world.
—J. I. Packer, *Knowing God*[1]

I think of a life dream. What do you really want? Maybe it's something that you want to have. Maybe it's something you want to do. Maybe it's something you want to happen.

Maybe you are praying and dreaming to get into the right college. If you can just get into that school, life will be good. You will be satisfied. Or, you are single and praying for the right person. You are praying for God's man to show up and capture your heart. You are praying for God's woman to walk into your life and make your knees go weak. Perhaps you think he's arrived, and you can't wait for him to pop the question. Or you're convinced that she's the one, and you are praying she'll say yes.

Maybe you are a little older and you are dreaming about your career. You are praying for a certain business venture to take off. You are working toward a dream position and praying for the right timing and circumstances. Maybe you have one of those BHAGs (big hairy audacious goals) they spoke about at your yearly sales conference. You are dreaming of great accomplishments so you can move to a more influential position and set some bigger audacious hairier goals (the hairy part never appealed to me).

Does your dream have something to do with your health? You can't remember what it was like to feel well and you're yearning for a stretch of good health. Maybe your dream involves your marriage, your children, or your grandchildren.

Whomever or whatever, you want it so badly that you can taste it.

Isn't it exciting and invigorating to dream? But here is the tough question: What happens if God says no? What happens if your dreams and God's will do not match?

There are many things we don't need to pray about doing or not doing. God's *revealed will* is laid out clearly in Scripture. God is rather "black and white" on his do's and don'ts. But God's *specific will* may not be so obvious. For example, I knew that I was supposed to marry a Christian (God's revealed will), but Scripture didn't tell me God's specific will. "Thus saith the Lord: 'You, Ron Moore, are to marry Lori Roth.'" That was certainly my dream, desire, and fervent prayer. I remember Lori saying one day, "I prayed that if I married anyone from Perry (our little town in Oklahoma) it would be you."

My first reaction was "Yes!!" But then I got to thinking. Perry is a very small town. Had she broadened the scope to Oklahoma, or the United States, or the world, I would have felt more encouraged. I was one of just a few people who were over eighteen years old with a full set of teeth who didn't drive a pickup with a gun rack full of guns. (If anyone from Perry is reading this, I'm joking. Perry is a great town. Put the gun down, slowly.)

I am so thankful that God said yes to my prayer regarding Lori. But not every dream I've had has worked out that way. So, back to my earlier question, how are we to respond when

God says no? How does God ignite a disappointed heart? To answer that question, let's consider a time in David's life when he received an unexpected answer from God.

DAVID'S GREAT REQUEST

In 2 Samuel 7, David was enjoying a time of blessing. Finally, he was settled in his palace. Years of running from Saul and more years of being king over only half the kingdom were behind him. It was time to move the united nation forward.

Israel was experiencing a time of peace. God gave David rest from all of his enemies. That had to feel good. No battering rams trying to knock down the gates. No flaming arrows flying through the air. No watching young soldiers die on the battlefield. Israel had not always been at peace and, for sure, wars would come again. But at this time, Israel was at peace. Best of all, the ark of the covenant, a physical reminder of God's person and presence, was back in Jerusalem. The Philistines possessed it for a time, but now it was back in the hands of its rightful owners. Israel was experiencing good things from God's hand.

Such times are great, aren't they? You know it's not the way things have always been and not the way they will always be, but even when we know things won't be like that forever, such times are welcomed and thoroughly enjoyed.

Picture a warm, paneled room. It smells like cedar. A fireplace is along one wall. As David sits alone in his easy chair and watches the logs crackle in the blaze, he dreams about all he wants to accomplish for God. He has more years behind than in front of him and there are still some important things he wants to achieve. Not selfish goals. Instead, he dreams about what he wants to make happen for God.

As David dreams, his mind goes to that object that represents God's presence—the ark of the covenant—presently housed in a tent. He looks around at his beautiful palace and contrasts the house he has built for himself with the location of the ark. David says to himself, "That's not right." So, he calls for Nathan, a prophet of God, a trusted friend, and advisor. He tells Nathan, "Here I am living in a palace of cedar, while the ark of God remains in a tent. Nathan, it's just not right. Look at the beauty and warmth of our surroundings, and the ark is outside in the cold. I need to build a great temple to house the ark."

Nathan agrees and says, "Whatever you have in mind, go ahead and do it, for the Lord is with you." After a period of time, I can picture Nathan getting up, and without saying a word, touching David's shoulder on his way out of the room, and leaving the king alone to dream.

David's Great Request—Denied!

That same night God speaks to Nathan, saying, "Go and tell my servant David, 'This is what the LORD says: Are you the one to build me a house to dwell in?'"(2 Sam. 7:5). The same story, recorded in 1 Chronicles, is reported in a much more straightforward way: "That night the word of God came to Nathan, saying: Go and tell my servant David, 'This is what the LORD says: You are not the one to build me a house to dwell in'" (1 Chron. 17:3–4). God was very clear: David, regarding your dream and desire—the answer is no.

God Will Always Answer Our Prayers

God will always answer our prayers; sometimes his answer is no.

"No, David, you are not the one to build me a house to dwell in."

"No, he or she is not the person for you to marry."

"No, that's not the college I want you to attend."

"No, this is not the position I want you to have."

"I know that it's disappointing. I know that it's heartbreaking. But you have to trust me. It's not my will. It's not my purpose. It's not my plan for you."

You say, "Well, my God's not like that! He always gives me what I want if I ask with the right motives. David must have asked with an impure heart. I bet that he really wanted the temple to be all about him." Nice try, but that was not the case with David. His heart was in the right place.

> My father David had it in his heart to build a temple for the Name of the LORD, the God of Israel. But the LORD said to my father David, "Because it was in your heart to build a temple for my Name, *you did well to have this in your heart.* Nevertheless, you are not the one to build the temple, but your son, who is your own flesh and blood—he is the one who will build the temple for my Name."
> —1 Kings 8:17–19, italics added

David's motives were pure; still the answer was no. God said, "David, you're a warrior, not a builder. The house will be built by your son, but not by you." David's warm dreams by the fire ended with a cold blast of disappointment. Ever been there? Are you there now?

Two Questions That Follow a Denied Request

When experiencing disappointment, there are two questions you have to deal with: Can you *trust* God? This is the theological question. The answer is easy. God is the almighty Maker of heaven and earth. He sent his Son to die for our sins. Sure, he can be trusted.

Can *you* trust God? That one's a little harder. We know he can be trusted, but do *you* trust him? Can *you* trust him when the answer is no? Can *you* trust him with your disappointed heart? Can *you* trust him with your shattered dreams?

At the end of a bloody battle during the Civil War, someone found the following prayer folded in the pocket of a deceased Confederate soldier:

> I asked for strength, that I might achieve;
> I was made weak, that I might learn to humbly obey.
> I asked for health, that I might do greater things;
> I was given infirmity, that I might do better things.
> I asked for riches, that I might be happy;
> I was given poverty, that I might be wise.
> I asked for power, that I might have the praise of men;
> I was given weakness, that I might feel the need of God.
> I asked for all things, that I might enjoy life;
> I was given life, that I might enjoy all things.
> I got nothing I asked for, but everything I had hoped for.
> Almost despite myself, my unspoken prayers were answered.
> I am, among men, most richly blessed.

God will always give us what we need, but it may not always be what we want. We may not understand his answer at the time, but as the soldier's prayer powerfully reminds us, God's response is always for our best.

Prayer Denied: An Instructive Response

Now, here is the issue: When God declines our request, how do we respond? David's reply is so instructive. Take the time to read the passage below slowly and reflectively. Don't forget, God has just told David no, regarding his great dream and desire.

> Then King David went in and sat before the LORD, and he said: "Who am I, O Sovereign LORD, and what is my family, that you have brought me this far? And as if this were not enough in your sight, O Sovereign LORD, you have also spoken about the future of the house of your servant. Is this your usual way of dealing with man, O Sovereign LORD?

> "What more can David say to you? For you know your servant, O Sovereign LORD. For the sake of your word and according to your will, you have done this great thing and made it known to your servant.

> "How great you are, O Sovereign LORD! There is no one like you, and there is no God but you, as we have heard with our own ears. And who is like your people Israel—the one nation on earth that God went out to redeem as a people for himself, and to make a name for himself, and to perform great and awesome wonders by driving out nations and their gods from before your people, whom you redeemed from Egypt? You have established your people Israel as your very own forever, and you, O LORD, have become their God.

"And now, LORD God, keep forever the promise
you have made concerning your servant and his
house. Do as you promised, so that your name will
be great forever. Then men will say, 'The LORD
Almighty is God over Israel!' And the house of your
servant David will be established before you.

"O LORD Almighty, God of Israel, you have revealed this to your servant, saying, 'I will build a
house for you.' So your servant has found courage
to offer you this prayer. O Sovereign LORD, you
are God! Your words are trustworthy, and you
have promised these good things to your servant.
Now be pleased to bless the house of your servant,
that it may continue forever in your sight; for you,
O Sovereign LORD, have spoken, and with your
blessing the house of your servant will be blessed
forever."

—2 Samuel 7:18–29

God ignited David's disappointed heart with trust. Note
the number of times that David refers to God as "Sovereign
LORD." David confesses that God is in control. David says,
"You are God and I am not. You know the beginning from
the end. You know what is best." Some people go through life
paralyzed by what God has withheld. Not David. Look again
at 2 Samuel 7:28–29. He moves from what God has withheld
to what God has given.

I am guessing that there is an area of your life in which
God has responded, "No." Maybe, like David, you know why.
Something has happened in the past to disqualify you from
your dream. Here are your options: You can run from God;
you can accuse God of not caring; or you can accept his plan
for you. David not only accepted God's plan, he believed in
God's promise that one day his son Solomon was going to

build the temple. So David used his time and energy to prepare the way for Solomon.

> David said, "My son Solomon is young and inexperienced, and the house to be built for the LORD should be of great magnificence and fame and splendor in the sight of all the nations. Therefore I will make preparations for it." So David made extensive preparations before his death.
>
> —1 Chronicles 22:5

I love David's response! As soon as some people hear God say no, they take their marbles and go home. Look again at what David did. He "made extensive preparations before his death." He knew that he would never see the temple, but his heart was ignited by trusting God's promise. So instead of sulking in disappointment, he used his knowledge and experience to help his young and inexperienced son fulfill the dream. When we, like David, realize that our dreams should be God's dreams, then we are willing to play whatever role he has for us, and at that moment, God ignites our disappointed heart.

"He Relies on the Troughs"

In C. S. Lewis's *Screwtape Letters*, Screwtape, the senior devil, describes difficult times in life as "troughs." His instruction to the junior devil about "troughs" is very instructive to us as well:

> Now, it may surprise you to learn that in [God's] efforts to get permanent possession of a soul, He relies on the troughs even more than on the peaks; some of His special favourites have gone through longer and deeper troughs than anyone else. The reason is this. To us a human is primarily food;

our aim is the absorption of its will into ours, the increase of our own area of selfhood at its expense. But the obedience which the Enemy demands of men is quite a different thing. One must face the fact that all the talk about His love for men, and His service being perfect freedom, is not (as one would gladly believe) mere propaganda, but an appalling truth. He really *does* want to fill the universe with a lot of loathsome little replicas of Himself—creatures whose life, on its miniature scale, will be qualitatively like His own, not because He has absorbed them but because their wills freely conform to His.

. . . Our cause is never more in danger than when a human, no longer desiring, but still intending, to do our Enemy's will, looks round upon a universe from which every trace of Him seems to have vanished, and asks why he has been forsaken, and still obeys.[2]

Scripture never says that a life following hard after Christ will be free from difficult times. In fact—this may not be the news you want to hear—a person following hard after Jesus will—not may, but will—experience some hard times. No one seeks dark valleys. But ready or not, here they come. In this life there will be "troughs."

In his book *The Faith*, Charles Colson has an excellent discussion regarding the inevitable sufferings of the Christian life. Based solidly in Scripture and illustrated with stories of real people, Colson says that "suffering belongs to our calling as Christians." Regarding the inevitability of tough times, he writes,

This is why easy-believism, the prosperity gospel, is so abominable: it sets a person up for a terrible fall when the first hardship comes, as it will. Whatever glimmer of faith the person might have may well be snuffed out.[3]

Then Colson concludes,

So the real question is not whether we will suffer but how we will react to adversity when it comes. We can see it as a miserable experience to be endured, or we can offer it to God for His redemptive purposes.[4]

David had his share of difficult times and deep disappointments. In Psalm 42, he asks himself, "Why are you downcast, O my soul? Why so disturbed within me?" Then he provides his own counsel: "Put your hope in God, for I will yet praise him, my Savior and my God" (Ps. 42:5–6). Whatever you are going through today, even if your soul is "downcast" and "disturbed," I invite you to join David is his prayer: *O God, my hope is in you. O my God, I will praise you!*

"I Desperately Want What I Have"

I don't know what God has held back from you that has left you disappointed. But I do know that the pain of an unmet expectation is real and deep. Lori and I have a friend who, with her husband, has prayed and prayed for a child. For whatever reason, to this point, God has said no. Her following thoughts are powerful and instructive:

You never think that "you" are going to be the one that struggles with infertility. . . . Every girl grows up dreaming of her wedding, living in a house with children, and living happily ever after. Once you find yourself in the midst of the tests and doctor appointments, you would never think that this possibly couldn't work . . . especially as a Christian. And when the outcome isn't what you expected, the first time, the second time, and so on, the hope starts to fade. You want to believe that God is big enough to do this—it has happened four billion times before, right? And then you begin to wonder. They say children are a blessing from God, so what did I do not to deserve the blessing? Why am I not worthy of this blessing?

Women tend to connect around their children or their pregnancy/delivery experience. Of course they do, because the majority have experienced childrearing firsthand. But how do I relate to that? There is *no way* I can enter into those conversations. I can't relate to the physical changes, emotional changes, or any part of pregnancy. I was pregnant once, for two weeks, and didn't even know it because the test was two weeks after the procedure. So, the day after Mother's Day—the first one I celebrated with true hope and expectation, I found out that I was in the process of miscarrying. One of my good memories of this experience is when [my husband] sent me sympathy flowers in memory of these children lost.

In 1 Samuel 1:10 as Hannah dealt with this issue, Scripture says, "in bitterness of soul Hannah wept much and prayed to the Lord." Yes, yes, and yes. You can be very bitter at times. Bitter to God, your husband, your family and friends. You cry *a lot*!! And you feel like you have prayed your heart out. Actually, you get sick of praying the same prayer over and over again: "Lord, please give us a child."

I finally had to ask [my husband] to stop praying that during our "before dinner" prayer. I couldn't stand to hear it anymore . . . four years with the same exact prayer is a long time.

There is great aloneness in infertility. No one knows what to say or what not to say. Usually an "I don't know what to say or do" is the best thing to offer someone struggling with infertility.

Infertility involves great grief and is a grieving process. I have found the way to deal with that grief is to understand that God is sovereign. He doesn't make mistakes; he doesn't need a do-over. "Oops" isn't a word in his vocabulary. He also doesn't waste a minute of whatever trial we find ourselves in.

We all have scars. Some of them are quite large and sometimes hidden—out of the view of the naked eye. This experience has refined my faith like fire refines gold. I wouldn't trade it for the world, because it has made me who I am in Christ. Someone once said to me, "I don't understand; you didn't get what you wanted in the end." My response was, *"Yes, but I want what I have. I desperately want what I have."*

Father, it is difficult to wait on our deep desires. It is very difficult to accept when you say no to the longings of our heart. But, Father, help us to accept what you want for our lives. And help us to desperately want what we have.
In Jesus' name.
Amen.

Chapter 11

Igniting an Empty Heart

"Why do I have three Super Bowl rings," Brady asked, "and still think there's something greater out there for me? I mean, maybe a lot of people would say, 'Hey man, this is what it is.'
I reached my goal, my dream, my life. Me, I think, 'God, it's got to be more than this.'
I mean this isn't, this can't be what it's all cracked up to be."

—Tom Brady
quarterback of the New England Patriots

Hang on tight—you're riding in a runaway mine car with Indiana Jones, sliding down the steep embankments; diving under a closing metal door laced with spikes; walking through dark caves filled with big crawling spiders and slithering snakes; turning a round rock that opens a cave wall; and there in the middle of the room on a pedestal illuminated by a mysterious light is a box. You approach the box . . . slowly . . . and you break the rusted ancient lock, open the lid, and oh no, the box is empty! Someone beat you to the treasure!

Many people go through life with all its thrills, spills, and excitement only to discover the box they have been searching for is empty. The promised treasure is missing. The satisfaction the job was supposed to bring is not to be found. The romance that knocked you off your feet breaks your heart. The bigger, better, and faster toys just don't fill the emptiness. We finally get the big corner office, but our heart is as empty as ever. That's what happened to Jeff Komlo.

THREE STORIES OF COMPLETE EMPTINESS

Jeff Komlo

Jeff Komlo had it all, or so it seemed. A standout athlete in high school, Komlo began his college career at Delaware as a walk-on quarterback and by his sophomore season was the Blue Hens starter. Standing 6'4", handsome and personable, Komlo was the big man on campus. "There was just this air, this presence Jeff put forward," said Ted Kempski, then the Blue Hens' offensive coordinator. "All the coaches thought the same thing: This guy's got it." Teammate K. C. Keeler said, "He was larger than life."

Every year Komlo improved. As a senior he led Delaware to the Division II national championship game and won All-American honors. In his three years as a starter, he passed for 5,256 yards and set over a dozen school passing records.

Toward the end of his four years at Delaware, Komlo started dating Jennifer Aldrich. She described the superstar treatment Komlo received. "Jeff cut to the front of every line. He never paid for a beer. He had girls writing his papers. The local merchants would do his dry cleaning or make his travel arrangements for free. I guess it's like this everywhere: When you're the star quarterback, you're like a god."

Komlo was the ninth-round draft pick of the Detroit Lions in 1979. He became a starter as a rookie when incumbent quarterback Gary Danielson had knee surgery in the preseason. Although the Lions had a dismal season, Komlo set a team rookie record throwing for 2,238 yards. After the season he and Jennifer were married.

Komlo never started another NFL game after his rookie season. When the journeyman quarterback retired he successfully transitioned into business, eventually cofounding a management consulting firm called Bolton Capital. In 1989 the Komlos moved into a seven-thousand-square-foot house in Bryn Mawr, Pennsylvania, and started raising the first of their four daughters. By the mid-90s their extravagant lifestyle, with country club memberships and vacation homes, was costing around $40,000 each month.

By early 2000, Jeff told Jennifer their marriage was over and that he had a girlfriend. In a series of incidents including DUIs, domestic violence, drugs, arson, and financial fraud, Komlo began what some called a "descent into darkness." He began his run from the law. His daughters nicknamed their missing father Osama. By the end of the summer of 2005, Komlo was featured on the Web site of the TV program *America's Most Wanted.* After that, he escaped to Greece.

At 3:00 A.M. on Saturday, March 14, 2009, Komlo's life came to an end when the car he was driving crashed into three cars before coming to a halt in southern Athens. Komlo was thrown through the windshield and died of a cranial fracture. He was fifty-two years old.[1]

How can you have it all and have nothing at the same time? How do you deal with an empty heart?

Vicki Van Meter

Vicki Van Meter was an amazing young woman. She began taking flying lessons at only ten years of age. At eleven, with an instructor by her side, Van Meter flew a single-engine Cessna 172 from Maine to California. On the trip back home she was invited to the Johnson Space Center. There she successfully landed the space shuttle simulator on her second try. Van Meter continued to fly, and her reputation grew through numerous television appearances and a White House invitation. She is one of forty-seven pilots featured in an exhibit called "Women in Flight: Portraits of Contemporary Women Pilots" that is now in the Smithsonian.

Ms. Van Meter served in the Peace Corps for two years in southern Moldova—a small European country bordered by Romania and Ukraine. She earned a degree in criminal justice and was working at an investigative firm. Everything was going her way, it seemed, until she ended her life at the age of twenty-six. Her brother said, "She was unhappy, but it was hard for her to open up about that and we all thought she was coping. This is really a shock because we didn't see the signs."[2]

How can you have it all and have nothing at the same time? How do you deal with an empty heart?

Tom Brady

Prior to the 2008 Super Bowl, *60 Minutes* did an exposé on the life of New England Patriots quarterback Tom Brady. The story focused on all of Brady's football accomplishments and his celebrity status off the field. But in response to his success, Brady echoed the thoughts of an empty heart.

"Why do I have three Super Bowl rings," Brady asked, "and still think there's something greater out there for me? I mean, maybe a lot of people would say, 'Hey man, this is what it is.' I reached my goal, my dream, my life. Me, I think, 'God, it's got to be more than this.' I mean this isn't, this can't be what it's all cracked up to be."

"What's the answer?" the interviewer asked.

"I wish I knew," Brady said. "I wish I knew. I love playing football and I love being the quarterback for this team. But at the same time, I think there are a lot of other parts about me that I'm trying to find."

How can you have it all and have nothing at the same time? How do you deal with an empty heart?

The "Empty Print" of the Heart

Blaise Pascal once wrote,

> What else does this craving, and this helplessness, proclaim but that there was once in man a true happiness, of which all that now remains is the empty print and trace? This he tries in vain to fill with everything around him, seeking in things that are not there, the help he cannot find in those that are, though none can help.[3]

We know that this world cannot satisfy the deepest longings of our hearts. The next purchase or victory or encounter brings momentary pleasure at best. And sooner or later, that desire for a temporary fix causes our castles to come crashing down around us. You can have it all and have nothing at the same time.

The apostle Peter preached the first sermon after Jesus was raised from the dead and ascended into heaven. Early in the sermon, Peter uses a quote by David to make his point.

> Men of Israel, listen to this: Jesus of Nazareth was a man accredited by God to you by miracles, wonders

and signs, which God did among you through him, as you yourselves know. This man was handed over to you by God's set purpose and foreknowledge; and you, with the help of wicked men, put him to death by nailing him to the cross. But God raised him from the dead, freeing him from the agony of death, because it was impossible for death to keep its hold on him. David said about him:

"I saw the Lord always before me. Because he is at my right hand, I will not be shaken. Therefore my heart is glad and my tongue rejoices; my body also will live in hope, because you will not abandon me to the grave, nor will you let your Holy One see decay. You have made known to me the paths of life; you will fill me with joy in your presence."
—Acts 2:22–28

The quote from David is found in Psalm 16. We don't know the specific circumstance that surrounded this prayer, but we do know that David was going through a very difficult time—a dangerous time—a time when he was running on empty. In this psalm, David says that his only refuge, his only place of safety, is God. Besides the Lord, he says, "I have no good thing." He makes the point that when we spend our lives running after "gods" our sorrows increase. Then in his prayer David gets to the point: "I have set the LORD always before me. Because he is at my right hand, I will not be shaken" (Ps. 16:8).

David speaks of a personal relationship with the living God. For David, the relationship is experiential. The Lord, David says, is "always before me." He is always with me. He never abandons me. I can count on him being with me at all times.

Psychologists talk about "attachment styles," ways in which children interact and depend on their parents. These attachment styles don't stop in childhood; they move into adulthood as well. One attachment style called "anxiousness" describes an uncertain or unreliable connection. People with the anxious attachment style desire closeness but worry that people might leave them because of their faults. They live on an emotional roller coaster. There are times they feel close and safe. Other times they feel distant and unprotected. They have a high anxiety about being abandoned and receiving insufficient love.

Do you ever wonder if you are on your own?

David knew that God was always with him. We can have that same assurance as well. We never have to worry about being abandoned. He is our protector and guardian. He leads the way for us. Remember David's words: "You have made known to me the path of life; you will fill me with joy in your presence" (Ps. 16:11). David's heart was filled with God.

But there is a reason David's heart was full. His heart was glad. He said, "My tongue rejoices; my body also will rest secure, because you will not abandon me to the grave" (Ps. 16:9–10). Do you hear what David is saying? David understands that this life is only temporal. Those who know God live beyond the grave. We all know that life is more than the measurement of our acquisitions. Deep within every living person is a desire for life beyond the grave. God has set eternity in our hearts (Eccl. 3:11). But the door to eternity cannot be opened on our own. Look again at David's words: "Therefore my heart is glad and my tongue rejoices; my body also will rest secure, because you will not abandon me to the grave, *nor will you let your Holy One see decay*" (Ps. 16:9–10, emphasis added).

One thousand years before the coming of Christ, David set forth the determining truth of the Christian faith—the resurrection of Jesus: "You will not let your Holy One see decay." Here is how Peter explains the words of David:

> Brothers, I can tell you confidently that the patriarch David died and was buried, and his tomb is

here to this day. But he was a prophet and knew that God had promised him on oath that he would place one of his descendants on his throne. Seeing what was ahead, he spoke of the resurrection of the Christ, that he was not abandoned to the grave, nor did his body see decay. God has raised this Jesus to life, and we are all witnesses of the fact.

—Acts 2:29–32

God ignites our empty heart with the empty grave. Our heart is ignited—in David's words, "filled with joy"—when we realize that God did not let Jesus stay in the grave but raised him to life. And because of the resurrection of Jesus, "you will not abandon me to the grave." There is life beyond the grave. Whether you are an Old Testament saint or an apostle or a member of the early church or living in the twenty-first century, the resurrection of Jesus is the event that changes everything. God ignites an empty heart with the certainty of an empty grave.

But why? Why does the resurrection's certainty ignite an empty heart?

The Bible tells us that when God created man there was an intimate personal relationship. Man spoke openly and freely with God just as we are speaking now. God surrounded man with everything that he needed. There was such purity and vulnerability that the Bible says the man and woman were both naked and felt no shame. We can't even imagine that now, but it was a time of complete purity.

Because God loved man so much he gave him the ability to make choices. God said, "All this is yours . . . you can eat freely and enjoy it all. But there is this one tree from which you cannot eat. There is this one thing you can't do. If you ever eat of the tree you will surely die." Adam and Eve failed that one assignment, and sin and death entered the human race. Life

150

after Genesis 3 is not the way it's supposed to be. Remember Pascal's words: "There was once in man a true happiness, of which all that now remains is the empty print." There is this desire in the heart of man to know God and live beyond himself, but sin makes us look for God in all the wrong places.

So God planned a way for man to find what he was looking for. Man sinned and sin deserved death, but God sent a substitute. Throughout the Old Testament he prepared and provided for his people. He instituted a system of substitution. The Old Testament believers sacrificed a lamb, bull, or goat knowing that the sacrifice was a stand-in for them. They also knew the sacrifice was not complete. They would have to repeat it year after year. The Old Testament believers knew of the promise of one who would come to make all things full and complete. But for that time, the sacrifice of an animal would be a substitute for their death.

Then God sent the Perfect Sacrifice. Jesus—fully God, fully man—went to the cross and died for your sin and mine. However terribly I have sinned, Jesus still thought I was worthy of his sacrifice. He forgives all who call on his name as their Substitute.

Now to be fair, forgiveness is not unique to Christianity. Buddhists prescribe the need for forgiveness because it prevents harmful emotions that disturb one's "mind karma." Hindus desire forgiveness because it is characteristic of one born of a divine state. Jews and Muslims teach forgiveness, but in both instances pardon is based on personal works.

Only in Christianity did God "take on flesh and live among us" (John 1:14). Only in the Christian faith did the Messiah come as fully God and fully man. In Jesus, God did for us what we could not do for ourselves. He died as the perfect, one-time-for-all-time sacrifice. As proof of God's power, he was raised from the dead. The apostle Paul explains it this way:

> And if Christ has not been raised, our preaching is useless and so is your faith. More than that, we are then found to be false witnesses about God, for we have testified about God that he raised Christ from the dead. But he did not raise him if in fact the dead are not raised. For if the dead are not raised, then Christ has not been raised either. And if Christ has not been raised, your faith is futile; you are still in your sins. Then those also who have fallen asleep in Christ are lost. If only for this life we have hope in Christ, we are to be pitied more than all men. But Christ has indeed been raised from the dead, the firstfruits of those who have fallen asleep. For since death came through a man, the resurrection of the dead comes also through a man. For as in Adam all die, so in Christ all will be made alive.
>
> —1 Corinthians 15:14–22

Had Jesus stayed in the grave, his death would have meant absolutely nothing to us. He would have been a man who simply died for a cause. But the resurrection changes everything. The certainty of the resurrection—the empty grave—is the only thing that can fill an empty heart. Without it, in Paul's words, our faith is futile and we are to be pitied more than all men. But with it, the resurrection changes everything. And it does even more than simply igniting our empty heart. It is the key to eternal life.

Ask God to ignite your empty heart with himself!

Father, I pray for those who do not know your Son, the resurrected Christ, as their personal Savior. Speak to their hearts as only you can do. Turn them from their current path to a journey toward you. Ignite their hearts with a burning passion to follow hard after you all the days of their lives.
In Jesus' name.
Amen.

Chapter 12

Igniting
a Heart of Grace

> The grace of God is love freely shown toward guilty
> sinners, contrary to their merit and indeed in defiance
> of their demerit. It is God showing goodness to persons
> who deserved only severity, and had no reason to expect
> anything but severity.
>
> —J. I. Packer, *Knowing God*

He was a thief. A common criminal. He spent his life taking what others had worked hard to earn. Some possessions he stole were cherished, irreplaceable family heirlooms handed down through generations. Some days he simply stole a loaf of bread or a piece of fruit to assuage his hunger. Who knows what happened in his early life. Perhaps it was the tragic death of his parents that put him on the streets to fend for himself. Maybe his parents taught him the "trade." But one day he was caught . . . red-handed . . . and the thievery ended . . . along with his life.

The punishment for his crime was death by crucifixion, a slow, agonizing death that allowed the criminal to reflect on his deeds until his last painful gasp of air. The ordeal began with beating and scourging. Then he was forced to carry his cross to the place of execution. On a hill called Golgotha he was forced to lie down on the beams. Soldiers stretched out his hands and drove a spike through his right wrist, then his left. They bent his knees slightly until his right foot was flat against the vertical beam. Then placing his left foot on top of his right the soldiers drove one more spike through both feet. He was fastened to the cross.

Two other men were going through the same ordeal that day, and one was drawing a good bit of attention. The thief's relatives had disowned him long ago, and his partners in crime were nowhere to be found. But a crowd had accompanied the man in the middle. He heard them call his name, "Jesus."

The thief had heard stories about Jesus. He touched blind eyes and made them see. Crippled men were able to walk. There was a story circulating that this Jesus had once called a dead man from the grave. Crowds gathered to hear him teach, and those in the thief's profession always knew where to find the crowds.

The thief was jolted back into painful reality as the soldiers lifted the cross and dropped it into a pre-dug hole. The sudden impact separated his shoulders and he prepared for the painful hours that stood between him and death. But his mind was taken away from the agony as he listened to the crowd yelling insults at Jesus. They showed no mercy even to the dying man. The other criminal, the one on the right of the man in the middle, was spewing abusive words. But in response to it all Jesus said, "Father, forgive them, for they do not know what they are doing" (Luke 23:34).

Then the thief said it, something he had been thinking about ever since he "worked" the crowds gathered around Jesus and heard him teach. Something he had been contemplating since he heard of the miracles. Something he began to believe as he watched Jesus go through the process of crucifixion. To the other criminal and all who could hear, he confessed, "We are punished justly, for we are getting what our deeds deserve. But this man has done nothing wrong." Turning his head toward Jesus he said, "Jesus, remember me when you come into your kingdom." And Jesus answered, "I tell you the truth, today you will be with me in paradise" (Luke 23:43).

Think about the scene. A criminal on a cross moments away from death. No opportunity to repay what he had stolen. No way to tell his victims he was sorry. No time to make restitution. Forgiven? Promised entrance into heaven? Can Jesus do that? Should Jesus do that?

Thank God he can! Thank God he does! Thank God for grace!

In a world where life and relationships are often based on performance, the truth of grace can be hard to understand and even harder to accept. Many struggle with the concept of grace. So as we close out our time together let's get a grasp on grace and then observe David as he puts it in action.

FOUR THINGS WE NEED TO KNOW ABOUT GRACE

In order for God to ignite our hearts with grace, there are four things we need to nail down. Here's the first one.

1. I have to understand and accept my moral condition.

The predominant worldview is that man—deep inside—is good. Certainly mistakes are made. Some drink too much, some get entangled in extramarital affairs, and some get caught in bad business deals, and, yes, sometimes other people get hurt. But there are reasons and excuses for all our problems. Our family history, background, environment, and even our DNA are used as reasons and excuses for our behavior. In spite of all our peccadilloes, we are inherently good. But the Bible explains man in a different way.

> The LORD saw how great man's wickedness on the earth had become, and that every inclination of the thoughts of his heart was only evil all the time.
> —Genesis 6:5

> The heart is deceitful above all things and beyond cure. Who can understand it?
> —Jeremiah 17:9

> For out of the heart come evil thoughts, murder, adultery, sexual immorality, theft, false testimony, slander.
> —Matthew 15:19

> As it is written: "There is no one righteous, not even one; there is no one who understands, no one who seeks God. All have turned away, they have together become worthless; there is no one who does good, not even one." "Their throats are open graves; their tongues practice deceit." "The poison of vipers is on their lips." "Their mouths are full of cursing and bitterness." "Their feet are swift to shed blood; ruin and misery mark their ways, and the way of peace they do not know." There is no fear of God before their eyes.
> —Romans 3:10–18

Inherently good? Far from it. We are morally bankrupt. David knew that he was a sinner from birth (Ps. 51:5). We are not sinners because we sin; we sin because we are sinners. And it is our sin that separates us from God. The prophet Isaiah wrote, "But your iniquities have separated you from your God;

your sins have hidden his face from you, so that he will not hear" (Isa. 59:2).

Either pride or ignorance of the truth causes us to refuse to admit our sinfulness. But until and unless we accept the hard truth of our sinfulness, our hearts will never be ignited by grace.

2. I have to accept and understand God's justice.

Universalism is the belief that at the end of the day all people will go to a "better place." Well, maybe not Hitler or Mussolini or the world's most demonstrably evil men, but for everybody else a loving God will welcome us all into his heaven. But here's the problem. The Bible says that God is a God of justice. He made it clear to Adam and Eve that their sin would bring death. And he is always true to his word. Sin deserves death. The prophet Nahum said that God is "slow to anger and great in power," then added, he "will not leave the guilty unpunished" (Nah. 1:3a). The apostle Paul made it clear that the "wages of sin is death" (Rom. 3:23).

A. W. Tozer addresses the danger of ignoring this attribute of God.

> But God's justice stands forever against the sinner in utter severity. The vague and tenuous hope that God is too kind to punish the ungodly has become a deadly opiate for the consciences of millions. It hushes their fears and allows them to practice all pleasant forms of iniquity while death draws every day nearer and the command to repent goes unregarded. As responsible moral beings we dare not so trifle with our eternal future.[1]

Can you imagine a judge, who has sworn to uphold the law, turning a blind eye to a person guilty of murder? "I know you have taken another person's life and I know what the law says, but you are free to go. Just don't kill anyone else." Absurd! Justice delivers the appropriate punishment on the lawbreaker. Justice demands that the penalty is carried out.

Sin is no joke with God. He hates it. He knows firsthand what sin has done to man. It is at the root of every murder, every word of slander, every war ever fought, every lie, every pain ever endured, every act of adultery, every broken family, every selfish action. Sin has separated man from God and it separates us from each other. And God doesn't wink at sin. He doesn't say, "I'll just pretend I didn't see that." He is just and demands judgment on sin.

3. I have to accept and understand my inability to fix my problem.

You and I are completely incapable of earning God's favor. Our sin has separated us from God and we cannot work our way back to him. Paul says,

> As for you, you were dead in your transgressions and sins, in which you used to live when you followed the ways of this world and of the ruler of the kingdom of the air, the spirit who is now at work in those who are disobedient. All of us also lived among them at one time, gratifying the cravings of our sinful nature and following its desires and thoughts. Like the rest, we were by nature objects of wrath.
>
> —Ephesians 2:1–3

Ancient pagans tried to earn God's favor by giving him more gifts and sacrifices. Others try to do it with some type of penance—beating themselves over the back or crawling on their hands and knees to Mecca. Today we are too sophisticated for that, so the modern worldview holds that you can earn your way to God by being good and by doing "religious" things. But catechism classes, baptism, Communion, church attendance, and giving to the homeless shelter are not enough to pay the penalty of our sin. In fact, Isaiah says that "all of us have become like one who is unclean, and all our righteous acts are like filthy rags" (Isa. 64:6). Our best effort is so far below God's standard it is like a "filthy rag."

Suppose I took my sixth grade daughter to a local college and somehow talked a professor into giving her a placement test for advanced calculus. "She is one smart little girl," I brag to the prof, "and I'd like to have her start accumulating some college credit." To humor me, he administers the test. However, the assessment doesn't go so well. She can't understand the questions, let alone decipher the answers. Her results don't even register on the lowest quartile. "Sorry," he says, "no credit." But I am not finished trying to get credit. "Come on, Doctor, Professor, sir, she tried so hard. Did you see the sweat pour from her little brow? She did her best. Please, give her some credit just for trying." The professor would respond to my plea, "Sir, her best effort didn't even come close; it didn't even register on the grading scale."

And so it is with us. Our best effort compared to God's perfect standard doesn't even come close. Compared to the expected perfection, it is like a "filthy rag." Paul says, "All have sinned and fall short of God's glory" (Rom. 3:23).

4. To understand grace, I must understand God's sovereign freedom.

Ancient pagans believed that the gods were bound to their worshippers out of self-interest. Today, many cling to a similar belief. They agree that we may not deserve God but that somehow God is obliged to help us. Modern man is like one of the

French thinkers who died muttering, "God will forgive me—that's his job." But the Bible is clear that God is independent. He needs no one or no thing. He is not beholden to man.

> I have no need of a bull from your stall or of goats from your pens, for every animal of the forest is mine, and the cattle on a thousand hills. I know every bird in the mountains, and the creatures of the field are mine. If I were hungry I would not tell you, for the world is mine, and all that is in it.
>
> —Psalm 50:9–12

Paul made this truth clear to the men of Athens:

> The God who made the world and everything in it is the Lord of heaven and earth and does not live in temples built by hands. And he is not served by human hands, as if he needed anything, because he himself gives all men life and breath and everything else.
>
> —Acts 17:24–25

God is not bound to show us favor. He is not obliged to pity us or pardon us. The only thing that God is obliged to do is judge us for our sin. The amazing thing about grace, then, is that it originates and proceeds from God, who has the freedom not to be gracious. J. I. Packer explains it this way:

> Only when it is seen that what decides each man's destiny is whether or not God resolves to save him from his sins, and that this decision which God need not make in any single case, can one begin to grasp the biblical view of grace.
>
> The grace of God is love freely shown toward guilty sinners, contrary to their merit and indeed

in defiance of their demerit. It is God showing goodness to persons who deserved only severity, and had no reason to expect anything but severity. We have seen why the thought of grace means so little to some churchpeople—namely, because they do not share the beliefs about God and man which it presupposes. Now we have to ask: why should this thought mean so much to others? The answer is not far to seek; indeed, it is evident from what has already been said. It is surely clear that, once man is convinced of his state and need are as described, the New Testament gospel of grace cannot but sweep him off his feet with wonder and joy. For it tells how our Judge has become our Savior.[2]

The Great Cost of Justice

Henri Latour was a real-life Sherlock Holmes, a scrupulous detective who always seemed to get his man. Latour became a living legend, and while stories of legends are often enhanced and embellished, the remarkable truth surrounding his last case was nothing less than remarkable.

A suspect had already been taken into custody when the master sleuth was called to the scene of a brutal crime—the murder of an elderly couple. After surveying the scene Latour told the authorities they had arrested the wrong man. He assured the police that critical pieces were missing from the puzzle. He would find the pieces and the true criminal. So began the brilliant track-down. Latour gathered and assembled the evidence one bit at a time. And citizens were comforted to know that Latour was on the case and closing in.

In the weeks that followed he accumulated all the needed evidence to clear the man the police had apprehended. The police wanted to keep their man in custody just in case Latour was wrong. But he assured them that he was not wrong and that an innocent man should not be forced to pay for the crimes of the guilty.

Latour continued his search. He continued to gather critical evidence—a patch of tweed, a smudge on a railing. Then one day the search ended. At the end of the long search, Latour found his man. The trial was short. Latour was on hand to testify. The verdict was "Guilty!" The judge commended Latour. The newspaper put the story on the front page. But this was Latour's last case. He retired, without explanation, and went into seclusion.

Everyone agreed that Henri Latour's last case was brilliant. Yet, the detective would live the final years of his life as a hermit in a little cottage in a secluded French village. Only after his death would the reason for his secret come to light. When the last puzzle piece was put in place, the detective was trapped by his uncompromising sense of justice. The innocent stranger he had set free was just that, an innocent stranger. But the evidence he so carefully collected led him to the arrest and conviction of his own son![3]

God's uncompromising justice demands that sin receives the penalty of death. So God, by his grace, chose to place that sin on his Son. Not because the Son was guilty; but because he was innocent, and only a perfect sinless sacrifice could suffice the justice of God. So the Father placed our sin on his Son. Jesus "bore our sins in his body on the tree" (1 Peter 2:24). On the cross Jesus paid the penalty for us, taking on the wrath of God. God's justice was satisfied by the death of his Son.

> We all, like sheep, have gone astray, each of us has turned to his own way; *and the LORD has laid on him the iniquity of us all.*
> —Isaiah 53:6, italics added

God made him who had no sin *to be sin for us.*
—2 Corinthians 5:21a, italics added

God imputed (attributed or assigned) my sin to Jesus. And on the cross the perfect Son—God in the flesh—paid the penalty for my sin by his death. And now God imputes the righteousness of the resurrected Lord Jesus to me. He takes my sin away and gives me a right standing before him! Paul explains, "For just as through the disobedience of the one man the many were made sinners, so also through the obedience of the one man the many will be made righteous" (Rom. 5:19).

Grace, in the words of the Princeton theologian Benjamin Warfield, is "free sovereign favor to the ill-deserving." And once we experience God's grace, we desire to show grace to others. This sovereign favor is beautifully illustrated in the man after God's own heart.

King Saul and his son Jonathan were dead and now David was the ruler of all of Israel. In 2 Samuel 8, the Lord gave David victory wherever he went. He "reigned over all Israel, doing what was just and right for all his people" (2 Sam. 8:15). As chapter 9 opens, David and Israel are experiencing a time of peace. In the time of David and throughout the history of monarchies, when a new king took over a throne the entire family of the previous king was put to death. The new regime wanted to ensure that the family of the previous king did not start a revolt or rebellion. Certainly any family of a king, even a former king, has influence, and the most expedient thing to do was to put them to death and therefore out of the picture. But David inquired about Saul's family for a different reason. He asked, "Is there anyone still left of the house of Saul to whom I can show kindness for Jonathan's sake?" (2 Sam. 9:1). The word *kindness* is a translation of the Hebrew word *hesed.* It describes a loyal love, an unfailing love, an unconditional love—in one word—grace.

Jonathan had been killed in battle with his father. In their late teens and early twenties, he and David had developed a very close friendship (see chapter 1). Saul hated David and made it his life's goal to put him to death. But Jonathan "became one in spirit with David, and loved him as himself" (1 Sam. 18:1). While Saul tried to kill David, Jonathan protected him and helped him escape. In return, Jonathan asked David for this agreement.

> "But show me unfailing kindness like that of the LORD as long as I live, so that I may not be killed, and do not ever cut off your kindness from my family—not even when the LORD has cut off every one of David's enemies from the face of the earth." So Jonathan made a covenant with the house of David, saying, "May the LORD call David's enemies to account." And Jonathan had David reaffirm his oath out of love for him, because he loved him as he loved himself.
>
> —1 Samuel 20:14–17

Now, years later, David is making good on the promise. He asks if anyone is still alive from Saul's household so that he can keep the covenant made with Jonathan.

> Now there was a servant of Saul's household named Ziba. They called him to appear before David, and the king said to him, "Are you Ziba?" "Your servant," he replied. The king asked, "Is there no one still left of the house of Saul to whom I can show God's kindness?" Ziba answered the king, "There is still a son of Jonathan; he is crippled in both feet."
>
> —2 Samuel 9:2–3

When Jonathan's son Mephibosheth was five years old his little life radically changed. Messengers raced into town and shouted the news that Saul and Jonathan had been killed in battle. The royal family was at risk, so his nurse scooped him up to flee for safety. In the frenzy, Mephibosheth fell and his feet were broken, possibly crushed. Due to the running and hiding, the injury was not properly attended to and he was crippled in both feet.

Eventually, Mephibosheth ended up in a place called Lo Debar at the house of a man named Makir. Makir was apparently a wealthy man who took it on himself to support the king's grandson. For the next years Jonathan's son lived in hiding, knowing that he would die should David discover his location.

Now fifteen to twenty years have passed. Mephibosheth is married and has a son named Mica. By this time he was no doubt confident that David either could not find him or had given up looking for him. But then one day, out of the blue, there was a knock on the door and Mephibosheth's heart sank. The king's men had tracked him down. He said goodbye to his family and prepared to go to Jerusalem to die.

When Mephibosheth appeared before David he got down on his knees and bowed before the king, expecting a death sentence to be pronounced. Instead, he heard these words:

> "Don't be afraid," David said to him, "for I will surely show you kindness for the sake of your father Jonathan. I will restore to you all the land that belonged to your grandfather Saul, and you will always eat at my table."
>
> —2 Samuel 9:7

There can be little doubt that Mephibosheth's self-worth was about a one on a scale from one to ten. He lived during a time when worth was based on performance. His dreams of being a great warrior like his father and grandfather had long ago been jettisoned. Unfortunately, in his day, Mephibosheth was a second-class citizen. As he knelt before David, his comments give us a picture into his heart. Mephibosheth bowed down and said, "What is your servant, that you should notice a dead dog like me?" (2 Sam. 9:8).

But David does not even acknowledge the question.

> Then the king summoned Ziba, Saul's servant, and said to him, "I have given your master's grandson everything that belonged to Saul and his family. You and your sons and your servants are to farm the land for him and bring in the crops, so that your master's grandson may be provided for. And Mephibosheth, grandson of your master, will always eat at my table." (Now Ziba had fifteen sons and twenty servants.) Then Ziba said to the king, "Your servant will do whatever my lord the king commands his servant to do." So Mephibosheth ate at David's table like one of the king's sons.
> —2 Samuel 9:9–11

What a great story of grace!

"Free Sovereign Favor to the Ill-Deserving"

Grace is something we don't deserve. We can do nothing to earn it. Grace is both unmerited and unjustifiable. Grace has nothing to do with our works. If it was based on works, Paul says, "grace would no longer be grace" (Rom. 11:6).

Mephibosheth was of no benefit to David. He was helpless. There was nothing he could do to earn David's favor. In fact, because of his heritage, he deserved death. But he received what he did not deserve. David provided land for Mephibosheth and every day he came to eat at the king's table. He was treated as one of the king's sons. That's grace!

The story of Mephibosheth eating at the king's table is the story of all those who receive God's grace. Just as Mephibosheth was born into a lineage that under David deserved to die, so each of us, born into the human race as sinners, deserve the punishment of that sin. Just as Mephibosheth was crippled in his feet, so sin has crippled our hearts. In our sinful state we are of no benefit to the holy God. Just as Mephibosheth lived far from the king, so our sin separates us from God and we are content to live at a distance. Just as Mephibosheth was shown undeserved favor and unconditional love, so are we. The guilty are pardoned. Those deserving death receive life. Just as Mephibosheth was given land and food at the king's table, so we have been given an eternal inheritance of heaven and an eternity with the King of Kings and the Lord of Lords.

Maybe you are still trying to work your way to God. You are still trying to be good enough. But you can never be good enough to earn the right to a relationship with the living God. Just how good would that be? Grace is for the crippled heart disabled by sin. God sent his Son to do for us what we could not do for ourselves. Paul reminds us of the great gift when he writes, "For it is by grace you have been saved, through faith—and this not from yourselves, it is the gift of God—not by works, so that no one can boast" (Eph. 2:8–9).

GOD'S AMAZING GRACE

When he was eleven years old he left school to become a hand on his father's ship. Thus began his life as a seaman. His early years can be best described by two words: rebellion and immorality.

169

After years of working as a crewman he bought his own ship. He and his crew would dock on the West African coast and capture men, women, and children. These people were then transported to the West Indies and America where they were sold as slaves. He was the captain of a slave ship—a cruel and immoral way of life.

In 1748 while returning to England his ship encountered a terrible storm. Thinking that he was going to die, he began reading a classic Christian work written by a Dutch monk named Thomas à Kempis. The message of the book, *The Imitation of Christ*, was used by the Holy Spirit to soften his hardened heart. He eventually trusted in Jesus Christ as his Savior.

He continued as a slave captain, trying to justify his work by improving conditions and holding worship services for the crew. But he could not justify life as a slave trader. He left the ship and went to work first as a clerk and then felt God call him into ministry. At the age of thirty-nine, he was ordained by the Anglican Church.

This man lived the rest of his life marveling at the grace of God. Before he died at the age of eighty-two, he was preaching and it is said that in the middle of his sermon he proclaimed in a loud voice, "My memory is nearly gone, but I remember two things: That I am a great sinner and that Christ is a great Savior!"

Today in a small cemetery in a churchyard in Olney, England, there is a granite tombstone over his grave with the following words written by the man himself:

> John Newton . . . once an infidel and libertine, a servant of slaves in Africa, was by the rich mercy of our Lord and Savior Jesus Christ, restored, pardoned and appointed to preach the Gospel which he had long labored to destroy.

John Newton wrote some other words and put them to music. This song, "Amazing Grace," is a testimony of God's work in the heart of every sinner. One of the verses of the song proclaims our eternal relationship with the living God by his grace:

> The earth shall soon dissolve like snow,
> The sun forbear to shine;
> But God, who call'd me here below,
> Will be forever mine.

It's God's amazing grace that saves lost and blind sinners like you and me. It's God's amazing grace that engages our hearts into an eternal relationship with the living God. It's God's amazing grace that ignites the heart with a burning passion to follow hard after him.

Heavenly Father, thank you for your amazing grace that saved a wretch like me. May I always be wowed by your grace. And as a grace receiver may I never neglect to be a grace giver.
In the matchless name of Jesus.
Amen.

Endnotes

Chapter 1: Igniting a Heart for God

1. Robert Boyd Munger, *My Heart—Christ's Home* (Downers Grove, IL: InterVarsity Press, 1986), 6.
2. Ibid., 28.
3. John Piper, *Desiring God: Meditations of a Christian Hedonist* (Oregon: Questar Publishers, 1986), 50.

Chapter 2: Igniting a Heart in the Sheep Pens

1. A. W. Tozer, *Whatever Happened to Worship?* (Camp Hill, PA: Christian Publications, 1985), 90–91.
2. *Christianity Today*, September 2008, "A Life Formed in the Spirit: Richard Foster's Disciplined Attention to Spiritual Formation began Early," interview by Mark Galli, 44.
3. According to www.snopes.com this story was written by S. I. Kishor and was originally published in a 1943 issue of *Colliers* magazine.

Ignite

Chapter 3: Igniting a Lonely Heart

1. www.barna.com, "Barna Finds Four Mega-Themes in Recent Research," December 3, 2007.
2. *Leadership Journal*, Fall 1996, vol. XVII, no. 4, 30.
3. Howard Markman, Scott Stanley, and Susan L. Blumberg, *Fighting For Your Marriage: Positive Steps for a Loving and Lasting Relationship* (San Francisco: Jossey-Bass, 1994), 233–234.
4. Clifford Notarius and Howard Markman, *We Can Work it Out: How to Solve Conflicts, Save Your Marriage, and Strengthen Your Love for Each Other* (New York: The Berkley Publishing Group, 1993), 132.

Chapter 4: Igniting a Stressed Heart

1. *USA TODAY*, Bob Nightengale, Monday, June 8, 2009.

Chapter 6: Igniting a Heart on Hold

1. C. H. Spurgeon, *The Treasury of David: An Expository and Devotional Commentary on the Psalms* (Fincastle, VA: Scripture Truth Book Company, 1984), vol. 1, 153.
2. Charles Colson, *Loving God* (New York: HarperPaperbacks, 1987), 33.
3. A. W. Tozer, *The Pursuit of God* (Camp Hill, PA: WingSpread Publishers, 2006), 17.

Chapter 8: Igniting an Obedient Heart

1. C. S. Lewis, *The Screwtape Letters* (New York: Macmillan Publishers Co., Inc., 1961), 56.
2. Ibid., 35.
3. Ibid., 60–61.

Chapter 9: Igniting a Fallen Heart

1. *Christianity Today*, September 2008, "A Life Formed in the Spirit: Richard Foster's Disciplined Attention to Spiritual Formation Began Early."
2. Dietrich Bonhoeffer, *Creation and Fall, Temptation* (New York: Simon & Schuster, 1959), 132.

Chapter 10: Igniting a Disappointed Heart

1. J. I. Packer, *Knowing God* (Downers Grove, IL: InterVarsity Press, 1973), 77.
2. C. S. Lewis, *The Screwtape Letters*, 56.
3. Charles Colson, *The Faith* (Grand Rapids, MI: Zondervan, 2008), 125.
4. Ibid.

Chapter 11: Igniting an Empty Heart

1. *Sports Illustrated*, June 15, 2009, vol. 110, no. 24, 62–73.
2. *Pittsburgh Post-Gazette*, March 19, 2008.
3. Blaise Pascal, *Pensees* (London: Penguin Group, 1966), 45.

Chapter 12: Igniting a Heart of Grace

1. A. W. Tozer, *The Knowledge of the Holy* (San Francisco: Harper & Row Publishers, 1961), 89.
2. J. I. Packer, *Knowing God*, 119–120.
3. Paul Aurandt, *Paul Harvey's The Rest of the Story* (New York: Doubleday Co. Inc., 1977), 144.